ADVANCE PRAISE

"This story of resilience will bring hope to parents faced with similar challenges. It should be a 'must-read' for mental health professionals, and I for one will recommend it to trainees as a book that will give them greater understanding and empathy for the families with whom they work. The balanced perspective of the book ... will do much to increase understanding and reduce stigma."

Paul Arnold, MD, PhD, FRCPC; Director, The Mathison Centre for Mental Health Research & Education; Alberta Innovates Translational Health Chair in Child and Youth Mental Health; Professor, Departments of Psychiatry and Medical Genetics, Hotchkiss Brain Institute, Cumming School of Medicine, University of Calgary

"*Hold on Tight* bravely documents a parent's journey in advocating for and supporting their two children with complex mental health presentations from childhood to adulthood."

Alexa Bagnell, MD, FRCPC; Chief of Psychiatry, IWK Health

"An open, insightful, and enlightening glimpse of a parent's life with two challenging and engaging children. ... If your life is connected to someone with mental health and/or cognitive difficulties, please read this book."

Mary Pat Armstrong, C.M., Founder and Chair, LIGHTS (partnership with Community Living Toronto that enables supportive housing for those with intellectual disabilities)

"An excellent journal and intervention manual for parents of neuro-diverse children."

Ken Shyminsky, Educator, advocate, and founder of NeurologicallyGifted.com

"I wish I could have read this in the early days with my son. It would have helped me to better understand what was required to navigate the medical system and schools, and how to better advocate in general. ... Regardless of a child's diagnosis, this book will help them tremendously. I would recommend it highly for any parent that has a child who is struggling."

Andrea Boulden, Senior Manager, Wealth Events, TD Bank, parent, and advocate

"A must-read for any family struggling to support their complex children or for those who know such a family. Through awareness comes compassion and a more inclusive world."

Amanda Matejicek, PhD, PCC, parent, business psychology consultant, and advocate

HOLD ON TIGHT

A Parent's Journey Raising Children with Mental Illness

JAN STEWART

BARLOW BOOKS
fine books for enterprising authors

ISBN 978-1-988025-97-1

Printed in Canada

Publisher: Sarah Scott
Book producer: Tracy Bordian/At Large Editorial Services
Cover design: Lena Yang
Interior design and page layout: Lena Yang
Developmental editing: Christina Palissio
Copy editing: Wendy Thomas

For more information, visit www.barlowbooks.com

Barlow Book Publishing Inc.
96 Elm Avenue, Toronto, ON
Canada M4W 1P2

For my heroes, Andrew and Ainsley,
and all the angels in their lives

CONTENTS

"Believe you can and you're halfway there."

–THEODORE ROOSEVELT

FOREWORD

Hold on Tight is a moving and compelling story of two siblings, their parents, and a family's journey shaped by mental health disorders. More than that, however, it's an intimate from-inside-the-family perspective of what often goes wrong in our current child and youth mental health system: The all-too-common and well-documented story of delayed diagnoses and long wait lists. Of reassurance from health care professionals instead of validation of parental concerns and concrete advice. Of lack of knowledge among health care providers on mental health problems of children and youth. Of roadblocks to successful transitions as children grow toward adulthood. Most importantly, though, it is an account of how two devoted and caring parents survive such a journey.

In many ways, the personal experiences Jan describes in this book are a testament to how *irrational* our mental health system is—and I say this as a health care professional with decades of experience in clinical practice, research, and exchanges with colleagues (mine is a from-inside-the-system perspective, if you will).

In contrast, a *rational* mental health system would have sufficient resources to achieve the best possible—or at least reasonable—mental health outcomes for the population at large, with particular focus on our children and youth. The system should include easy-to-access clinical services for those with mental disorders, prevention programs for those at high risk of developing a disorder, and a broad mental health promotion program to increase mental health literacy skills.

For such a system to work, it needs to be built on a foundation that is evidence based, incorporates patient values, and is derived from clinical-practice guidelines developed free from bias. Implementation means targeting and reaching those in need, delivering services that are faithful to the principles of the prescribed intervention, and having the ability to scale up to serve all citizens. Based on these indicators, it is all too clear that we do not yet have a rational mental health system for children and youth in Canada.

This book shares the hard-won solutions that Jan and her husband sought and created to help their children despite an irrational health care system. They found resources, educated others, and understood that the whole family was in it together. Not surprisingly, those are precisely the problems our mental health system needs to address.

Another problem our mental health system needs to address — powerfully illustrated by Jan's story — is that the current system seems geared to service the provider, not the family. Jan's accounts of Andrew and Ainsley remind us that *the patient is, in fact, the whole family* and that a family-centred approach should be the cornerstone of our mental health care system. Everyone in Jan's family suffered and needed understanding and support. That support was stitched together by Jan and her husband over time. How much better would the outcomes have been if this support were provided in the beginning in an organized and systematic way?

I wish I'd had this book when I started training some forty years ago. Navigating the mental health system, even a rational one, is challenging and can crush many a parent's spirits. The recommendations Jan provides in the last section of this book — how to survive the system — are so helpful. They are exactly what I counsel parents who have children and youth with complex and severe mental health problems such as autism, anxiety, depression, or ADHD. Jan's advice will resonate with, encourage, and embolden parents. This book also offers a unique opportunity for relatives and friends, health care providers and educators, and employers to see family life through those parents' eyes.

Stories bring understanding to adversity. This is a story of mourning, of challenges, and at the end, if not of complete triumph, of notable victories and of acceptance. At one point in the book, Jan's son Andrew says that he "would much rather have cancer and have my life on the line due to the cancer than live through what I went through. It really was the definition of Hell." Pause a moment and think about that.

Parents of children and youth with mental health problems who read this book will gain much. But Jan's story also speaks to a wider audience and a bigger issue. We — as a society and as health care professionals — must do better. We have to replace a flawed system with a rational one that provides equitable access to high-quality mental health care for the entire family.

Read this book and you will understand why that transformation is needed. Read this book and you will learn how we can accomplish it, together.

Dr. Peter Szatmari
Child and Youth Psychiatrist,
Hospital for Sick Children
Centre for Addiction and Mental Health
University of Toronto

PROLOGUE

I never thought I would live with fear in my own house. But when I came home one winter evening and found my seven-year-old daughter, Ainsley, barefoot in the snow, sobbing and shivering uncontrollably, I died inside. Her nine-year-old brother, Andrew, was having a rage, screaming as if he was possessed. He was punching holes in walls, ranting and swearing. His eyes were on fire. This usual gentle, loving boy had become a terrifying monster.

The day had started off calmly. I woke up at 6 a.m., as I did most weekday mornings, to get ready for work. I remember being preoccupied with two vastly different topics: the search that I was leading for a senior investment executive at a major Canadian pension fund, and researching Andrew's latest ritual of scab-picking. Andrew had recently started picking scabs all over his body non-stop, making them bigger and infecting them. He just couldn't seem to stop, and I was frightened, not only of his bizarre behaviour but of the possibility of his infecting and scarring his body. Preoccupied, I mechanically prepared the children's breakfasts and lunches and woke them. Andrew had opened a small scab on his arm that had been starting to heal but was now nearing double the size and was oozing. I put Polysporin and a Band-Aid on it and crossed my fingers that he could get through the day without causing further damage.

Andrew and Ainsley were eager to get to school. They were both making Valentine's Day cards in their classes. They were also excited about building a snow fort at school with their friends. As the sun came up, it was clear that the day would be ideal for that activity, with pale blue skies, a few wispy clouds, and temperatures in the –7 degree Celsius range. They made their beds, ate breakfast, got dressed, brushed their hair and teeth, and gathered their school bags with homework and lunches with my help. I left for work first to take the subway downtown to my office, while my husband, David, cleaned up and chatted with the children until the nanny started at 8 a.m. to walk them to school.

My day at work was packed full of meetings and calls. I met with the chief executive officer at the pension fund I was working with and interviewed three executives as potential candidates for senior positions at different companies. I had lunch with a colleague who was visiting Toronto from our firm's Zurich office and who made me laugh with his many questions about poutine.

That afternoon, I was able to take some time to research scab-picking. I called Andrew's psychologist and his psychiatrist to discuss whether the medications he was taking to counter his rituals were strong enough or whether he needed higher dosages or different medications and/or approaches. His rituals were elusive because they kept changing, seemingly every week. The week before, he had washed his hands multiple times an hour until they were raw and had started bleeding. The previous week, he couldn't complete any task without repeatedly counting to fourteen. He had started engaging in these rituals six months earlier, and they plagued every waking moment of his day. The scab-picking scared me because

it posed imminent physical danger to his body, and that fear propelled me to keep seeking answers and to find relief for him.

I had become accustomed to girding myself at the end of
the workday to prepare for the reality waiting for me at home. I
didn't know what shape each child would be in. Would Andrew
have hurt his neck due to his tic of continually throwing it back?
Would Ainsley have been sent to the principal's office again for
standing on her desk, interrupting others, or refusing to follow
directions? I called the nanny just before I left, who told me that
both children had had good days, were doing their homework,
and seemed happy. I allowed my body and mind to relax a bit.

David and I both got home at around 6 p.m., kissed the
children, and asked about their days. Ainsley was proud of her
behaviour that day and had gotten a gold star from her teacher.
Andrew had not made his scabs worse. The nanny had fed them
dinner right before we got home and was ready to go to a friend's
house. David and I had been invited to drop by a neighbour's
house to meet their new baby. Given the children's positive day,
we felt comfortable that they would be fine with us two houses
away for a short period.

Almost immediately after we left, Andrew started having a
rage. The rage had nothing to do with our absence and came out
of nowhere, as it usually did. We rarely knew what set a rage off —
the reasons seemed elusive. He screamed at the top of his lungs,
punched holes in walls, threw chairs, and swore repeatedly. He
looked like a demon who had morphed from a cheerful, loving
boy into the devil. Ainsley was terrified and didn't feel safe. She
ran out of the house in her nightgown with no coat or shoes. She
stood in the snow, weeping and trembling uncontrollably. This
wasn't Andrew's first rage — he had started having them the past
summer and they seemed to happen every other day. But this was
the first time we were not home to protect her.

Fifteen minutes after we left the house, David and I returned to check on the children. You can imagine my horror at finding my little girl in the snow, barefoot, freezing, and hysterical. You can imagine my shame at having put her in such a horrific situation. I wept inside not only for Ainsley, but for Andrew and for David and me as well. Would our lives ever be normal? Would we ever climb out of this morass?

I picked Ainsley up and enveloped her in my arms. I tried to soothe her and reminded her that the rages were Andrew's disorders speaking, not him. He couldn't control them. David carried a screaming and kicking Andrew down to the playroom, where we had replaced all the furniture with huge pillows so that he could punch and throw them without hurting himself. We switched children, and I waited near the playroom while David took Ainsley up to her bedroom to further calm her down, read to her, and comfort her.

As I waited for Andrew's rage to wind down, I silently thanked God for having David as a partner. I couldn't have asked for a better, more understanding husband; he was as frightened as I was but did not shy away from tackling these challenges and diving in to help. At the same time, I went into "ice mode": I steeled my body for the rage to end and seemingly felt nothing. These rages didn't last just five or ten or thirty minutes. They were sometimes two hours long and all-consuming. Life simply stopped.

After an hour and a half, Andrew's ranting finally transitioned from screaming into crying and whimpering, the sign that his rage was over. I hurried into the playroom and held him for a long time in a huge bear hug. He wept that the behaviour was not him and kept apologizing that he didn't mean anything that he had said and that he didn't want to hurt anyone. He pleaded and pleaded for help.

No one had been able to give us a name for Andrew's behaviour, and both David and I were desperate. And as heartbreaking as that evening was, what has stayed in my mind all these years is how terrified it felt to be living in a family with an abuser. And that abuser was not my son but his disorders.

INTRODUCTION

From the day that I was born, an idyllic life seemed planned for me. I was born in New York City to loving parents who soon moved to the suburbs to raise me and my younger sister in one of the best school districts in the country. We lived in a beautiful Georgian house, had a full-time housekeeper, enjoyed vacations in the sun, ballet and acting lessons, summer camps away, and, above all, a close-knit, happy family.

My father was a shopping mall developer who travelled across the United States the majority of each workweek, leaving my mother to largely raise us. This is not to say that my father wasn't there for us: he coached our softball and soccer teams, rarely missed a school concert or play, and played tennis with me each weekend. But he was twelve years older than my mother, and, in hindsight, I think having children was a shock to him. He was kind and loving but didn't really know how to relate to two daughters.

My mother, however, doted on us. As a former model and Broadway actress, she was tall and thin, extremely well read, and carried herself with a dramatic flair. She was ambitious for her children and instilled in us a tremendous work ethic. She knew how important it would be for both of us to become financially independent and self-sufficient, never needing to rely on a husband or anyone else for financial support. We studied for hours every afternoon and evening, following the expectations placed upon us by both our parents and by our high-pressure high school. We never questioned these expectations or viewed them as a burden. And we succeeded in just about everything we did.

In my senior year of high school, I applied for early admission to Northwestern University outside Chicago. With the taste of the Vietnam War in my mouth and the myriad of anti-war protests in my community, I was eager to leave the East Coast. I also wanted to study speech pathology, having been inspired by a neighbour in the profession who told me how she helped turn around people's lives. Northwestern had a renowned speech pathology program, and I fell in love with the university when I visited. It didn't hurt that the football player who took me around campus told me that I reminded him of Ali MacGraw from the recently released film *Love Story*! I joined a sorority, made two extremely close friends, had my first serious boyfriend, and graduated as one of the top ten students in my class. I spent a number of summers in France, living with French families and then working in both Paris and the southwestern region of the country, becoming fluent in the process.

While studying, I became inspired by one of my professors who was deaf. He taught me American Sign Language and encouraged me to pursue further studies in the field. This led me to obtain a graduate degree in deafness rehabilitation in New York. I worked briefly for a community service centre for the deaf, followed by two years as the assistant to the executive director of a national coalition lobbying for the rights of physically disabled individuals. I was even invited to the White House to interpret (into sign language) a meeting between then–First Lady Rosalynn Carter and a number of disability leaders.

These were heady civil rights days in the United States. It became apparent to me that a disabled person should ideally fill my role in advocacy to better represent the community. At the same time that I was coming to that realization, I was also becoming interested in developing my business skills. While I was unsure of exactly what I wanted to do, I knew that I sought broader career options with the potential to advance, likely in not-for-profit administration. I decided to obtain my MBA and moved back to New York to enrol at Columbia University. I surprised myself and particularly enjoyed my classes in finance, finding that I had a natural talent for analyzing and understanding the meaning behind numbers. This led me to pivot my career 180 degrees and join the prestigious U.S. bank J.P. Morgan & Co. on Wall Street upon graduation.

It was during this period that I met my future husband, David. I had met one of his best friends, Mack, on vacation in the Caribbean in 1984. Mack and he had met at their boarding school during high school and lived very near one another in Toronto. Several months later, out of the blue, Mack called to ask if he and his friend David could stay at my apartment one Friday night on their way to Atlantic City for the weekend. I of course said yes.

David was originally from Montreal but had been living in Toronto for the past three years. As soon as I met him, I knew that he was "the one." He was 6'2", thin and fit, with pale blue eyes and a smile that melted my heart. We went out to dinner and I showed them around my neighbourhood on the Upper East Side of Manhattan. We laughed continuously as they told me funny high school stories. And as I got to know David that evening, I became more smitten as he seemed kind, intelligent, and non-judgmental of others and had a great sense of humour. Family meant a great deal to him, as did friends. I could sense David flirting with me as much as I was flirting with him. After they left for Atlantic City the next morning, I hoped that he would reach out to me but wasn't sure.

About a month later, David sent me a letter spelled out in the sign language alphabet and invited me to Toronto. Our first date was spent over the New Year's weekend. I was hesitant to spend four full days with a date I hardly knew, but my fears quickly dissipated as he was so easy to be with and we talked non-stop.

David and I came from similar upper middle-class families with shared values of hard work, kindness, curiosity, and giving back to others. He loved to travel (albeit in a more rugged manner than I enjoyed) and to watch wildlife documentaries, as I did. He was not as ambitious as I was, but he was entrepreneurial and was interested in starting his own financial planning business. He provided me with needed balance that helped me to slow down my unrelenting pace and enjoy life more.

From that time on, we were as inseparable as we could be, given our distance. He called me every day. We flew back and forth to be with each other every other weekend. On one visit to Toronto that February, a nasty ice storm descended, and I spent five full days holed up in David's house until I could get a flight home. This allowed us to deepen our bond, and we spent hours playing board games, watching TV movies, cuddling, and laughing. We booked a holiday together on the Caribbean island of St. Croix shortly thereafter and found that we both enjoyed walking on the beach, snorkelling, and playing tennis. And importantly, he met my parents and spent time with them on every visit to New York. My normally judgmental mother made it clear to me that he was a keeper.

After having dated a number of men in my late twenties and early thirties, I had developed a six-month "up-or-out" rule: if a relationship wasn't progressing to the point of becoming permanent after six months, I felt that there was no future and it was time to move on. I mentioned this to David early on, and I remember that he oddly didn't react. But things progressed: he asked me to fly to Montreal to meet his mother and siblings one weekend. I was amused as I met them, as they all looked alike. They were accepting of me from the start and resoundingly approved of our relationship. He also brought me to his family cottage in the Laurentians another long weekend, where we swam, canoed, and relaxed with family and friends.

Exactly six months into our courtship, David came to New York for a regular weekend visit. His plane was delayed due to a flat tire, and he didn't arrive until shortly before midnight. As soon as he kissed me hello, he stepped out onto my tiny balcony in the pouring rain and proposed, just before the clock struck midnight. I guess he had been listening to my up-or-out rule! I was thrilled, although I immediately ran to the bathroom and threw up from excitement. I called my mother surreptitiously while he was taking a shower and whispered my news to her. She promised to keep the secret until David asked my father for his blessing the next day. We celebrated with champagne.

We were married exactly one year after we met. Our wedding was held at The Pierre, at the time a Canadian-owned hotel in New York City, which agreed to fly both the American and Canadian flags above their front doors that day. Mack was David's best man. That October morning was rainy and cool, but the sun came out after our celebration and we took a romantic carriage ride around Central Park. We left for our honeymoon the following morning on the island of St. John in the Caribbean and then settled into married life in Toronto. J.P. Morgan transferred me to its Toronto office, and my life continued on happily, as expected.

David and I decided to start a family one year later. David had always wanted children, and I knew that he would be an involved, loving father. I, on the other hand, had not thought much about motherhood. It was not something that I had craved before meeting David. With him as my partner, however, I wanted to have children. We knew that we had to get going as we were approaching our mid-thirties.

I easily became pregnant, and David and I began to plan for the future. I fervently wished for a healthy baby and envisioned passing on many of the values that my parents had instilled in me: the importance of confidence, independence, and ambition, with a strong sense of self and work ethic. I wanted our child to be a good, kind person who would champion the underdog. I also wanted them to have the best chance of succeeding by graduating from the best schools, learning multiple languages, and living and working perhaps in the United States or elsewhere. David similarly wanted a healthy baby and a happy, outgoing, successful child. He wanted our child to attend the same boarding school during high school that he had, travel, become independent and confident. He didn't care what they did as long as it provided a sense of achievement in life, and he hoped that they would enjoy a healthy social life with friends. We prepared for the baby's arrival by reading every book we could find, obtaining advice from family and friends, and shopping at baby stores for everything from a crib and change table to pastel wall hangings.

Our first child, Andrew, was born in July 1987. His birth was uneventful. Friends and family joked that he — of course — was born on his due date, as I was highly efficient and lived according to a tight schedule of activities and meetings. He was named after David's eldest sister, Andrea, who had tragically died of leukemia in her thirties. David called my mother before we drove to hospital, and she immediately flew into Toronto, arriving just ten minutes after the birth.

What I wasn't prepared for was the post-natal depression I faced. I had always been in control of my life, but I was now faced with a newborn and no knowledge of what to do. My mother could stay only a few days because my father was ill. I found myself at a loss, crying throughout the day and panicking as I waited for David to return home from the office. My depression was exacerbated by the fact that I was still new to Canada and did not yet have real friends of my own to lean on.

Recognizing the situation, my mother convinced us to quickly hire an experienced nanny. I returned to work four weeks later. This not only allowed me to regain control of my life and enjoy the intellectual stimulation that my job offered, but gave me the breathing room that I needed to be able to function. Some of our friends and family were horrified by my quick return to the office, but doing so gave me needed relief, lifted my depression, and made me a much better, more patient mother.

Shortly after Andrew was born, I joined the Toronto office of the global executive search firm Egon Zehnder. I had become intrigued with recruiting and realized that it was a much better fit for me than banking. I loved meeting with companies and making a significant impact on their success by finding the right executives and board members for them. It was a high-pressure environment with tight deadlines, but I loved it, and I marvelled at the fact that I was being paid to listen to senior executives tell me their intriguing life stories every day.

I looked forward to coming home to Andrew every evening and spending time with David and Andrew on weekends. Andrew slept through the night early on and was generally a happy baby, although both of us felt that something was different with him early on. He seemed to have no internal controls about when to stop feeding. We performed an experiment when he was about six months old in which we gave him as many bottles as he wanted; he quickly finished five full bottles and would have kept feeding had we let him. It scared and baffled us.

Watching our friends' babies and listening to them talk about their children's gurgling and chatter heightened my antenna about Andrew. Andrew refused to play in his crib. He didn't talk to himself. His hands and feet moved in circles constantly. He seemed to cry a lot and was difficult to soothe. We read and read books on normal developmental behaviour but couldn't find a name for what we were experiencing. We were concerned, but in spite of these behaviours and his non-stop bottle feeding, he was generally content. He beamed at others and was very social. I remember meeting a work colleague on the street one day with Andrew in his stroller; he told me that he had never seen a happier baby! I questioned myself about whether I was being overly worried and just needed to relax.

David and I had always discussed having two children, so that each would have a sibling to grow up with. Shortly after Andrew turned one year old, I became pregnant again. I enjoyed a healthy pregnancy, and I was psychologically and emotionally prepared for potential post-natal depression this time. Andrew's nanny was there to help and couldn't wait to take care of two children.

Ainsley was born in May 1989. Her birth was easy, and we named her after my mother's Broadway stage name. She was adorable, with reddish-blond hair and pale blue saucer eyes. We felt fortunate to have a boy and a girl and were content that our family was complete. We proudly showed them off and lavished them with attention and love, along with far too many toys, clothes, and books.

As cute as Ainsley was, however, she too exhibited some early troubling behaviours. While she was refreshingly easy as a baby compared to Andrew and was adorably impish and mischievous, she quickly spiralled out of control as a toddler. She was disruptive and couldn't sit still. She couldn't seem to focus. David's mother, who wanted the children to attend church one Sunday when we were visiting her in Montreal, asked us to leave after ten minutes after Ainsley started climbing over the pews.

We watched these cracks begin to show, but we had no benchmarks against which to compare the children's development. Even though I knew in my gut that both children faced challenges, our pediatrician repeatedly reassured us that they were fine and that I, as a "AAA-type person from high-pressure New York City," should relax. And so, like so many of our friends at the time, most of our conversations centred on how to optimize our children's rosy futures. We pondered not only which private schools to consider, but whether they should be educated in French and English, attend university in Canada or the United States, which camps to send them to, and which activities they should participate in. I had visions of Andrew becoming a world-class skier or Ainsley becoming a ballerina.

As the children's disorders became increasingly apparent, however, our dreams and our lives changed drastically.

part one

ANDREW

THE EARLY YEARS

When I look back at Andrew's first year, a number of troubling signs emerged early. One of the first things we noticed, in addition to his lack of self-control in feeding, was that Andrew never played in his crib when he woke up or "talked" to himself, as many babies do. Instead, he demanded that we immediately pick him up and feed him. Friends talked about their babies' joyful gurgling sounds and shared stories of them happily swatting at toys in their cribs and entertaining themselves. All Andrew did was cry. We consulted with our pediatrician and read a number of books that recommended behaviour modification techniques, including ignoring him for gradually longer periods so that he would learn to stop. Nothing worked: after three solid weeks of assiduously following their advice, Andrew's crying just kept getting worse. No one seemed to have an explanation, and the doctor assured us that this phase would pass. I was exhausted and frustrated that there was no easy answer.

Andrew's first year was focused on food ... overly focused. Our pediatrician had told us to feed him whenever he was hungry until he refused the bottle. But since he was never full, we made the decision to control his intake at scheduled times. To our surprise, we found that when we stopped feeding him, he was equally happy. It became clear that he lacked self-regulation skills even as a baby.

Andrew's insatiable feeding and crying weren't the only issues that the pediatrician told us not to worry about. When we asked our doctor about Andrew's habit of flapping his arms and continually making circular motions with his wrists, he told us that these reflexes were totally normal, even though it was apparent to us that his movements were significantly more frequent than those of our friends' babies. We later learned that these movements can be one of the risk markers for a number of neuro-developmental disabilities. At the time, however, we didn't know any better as new parents. Even though our intuition told us that his behaviour wasn't like that of other babies, we believed in our doctor and we never thought to challenge his advice.

As Andrew developed, he was a study in contrasts. He successfully hit his developmental milestones in the first year, from smiling and rolling over to sitting and crawling. He started walking at fourteen months. And he loved being with other people. He particularly enjoyed playing peek-a-boo, listening to music, and reading books. Puzzles entertained him, and he had several favourite stuffed animals. He was easily potty trained. We delayed moving him out of his crib because Ainsley was born at that time, but shortly after, he made the transition to a bed without a problem.

As a young toddler, Andrew didn't talk. When he wanted something, he would make repetitive bleating noises and sometimes point. We could often figure out what he was trying to say but not always. This would increasingly frustrate Andrew and us, leading to long crying bouts and more bleating. When we told him that it wasn't yet time to eat, he would nevertheless persevere and continue to bleat. At times, I felt like I would scream from frustration but I was careful never to show him anything but patience; this of course took a further toll on my fortitude.

Andrew did best when he followed a schedule. After dinner each evening, like many children, he had a bath, played with toys, and we read books together. Right before lights out at 7:30 p.m., I sang him a special lullaby. I had found a beautiful compilation of lullabies called *A Child's Gift of Lullabies* by Tanya Goodman. At the time, Andrew slept with a small teddy bear named Sydney that David's mother had brought him. I thought it would be perfect to sing him one of the songs on the album called "Lullaby for Teddy." The lyrics ask the child to close his eyes and then Teddy, who is very tired, will also go to sleep.

I thought that Andrew looked forward to this calming lullaby each evening. Only years later did he admit how terrified he had been of the lyrics, believing in his little mind that Teddy was never going to wake up and that he would die. Unbeknownst to me, he was traumatized so many nights, heightening his anxiety. When he told me, I felt like an awful mother.

When Andrew hadn't started talking by age two, we took him to a speech therapist. She counselled us not to be concerned and told us that his speech was delayed but still within acceptable parameters. Sure enough, within months he started talking and putting together sentences, catching up to his peers.

But even though he was becoming more independent in some ways, he continued to cling to me. He was happy to be with his nanny when I was at work, but whenever I was around, he stuck to me like glue. He wouldn't even go to David, who did everything that he could to try to spend time with him. This was hurtful to David and exhausting to me, wearing me down further. At least work provided a respite during the weekdays. The worst month for me was April, when David had to be at his office non-stop preparing clients' taxes, and I was alone with Andrew each weekend. I often felt like I was being smothered and couldn't get a break. We again consulted the doctor, who reassured me that Andrew was like any other child and that I needed to be less of a hyper-focused parent. Again as a first-time mother, I accepted his advice, acknowledging that I am indeed AAA in character in most aspects of my life. But I should have trusted my gut.

GROWING CONCERNS

As Andrew grew into a toddler, he was outgoing and cheerful. He sang songs all the time, loved playing with his little sister, made friends in the neighbourhood, and was generally very happy. He chatted up a storm, asked lots of questions, and displayed non-stop curiosity.

But his crying bouts continued. David and I remember taking him to a nearby shopping mall one Saturday. Andrew wanted a toy that we would not buy him. He ramped himself up into a full-blown tantrum, screaming at full volume, flailing his arms, and kicking the floor. We had read parenting books and talked to friends who told us to ignore the tantrums, so we walked away slightly while keeping him in our sights so that he was safe. Andrew didn't stop screaming. After about twenty minutes, David picked him up to carry him to the car. Security closely followed him out, concerned that he was kidnapping a hysterical child.

David and I became increasingly dismayed, finding again and again that Andrew did not follow expected childhood patterns or our friends' experiences with their children. He was constantly in motion and easily distracted. He couldn't seem to stick with one task, moving midway from colouring a picture to putting together a puzzle to jumping and singing. Our pediatrician, friends, and family kept telling us to calm down. They were like a broken record. My mother was the one exception. She trusted me and validated my concerns. But she was more worried about me falling apart than about Andrew's issues.

As he grew, Andrew continued to be overly focused on food and was gaining weight. David and I remember how disturbed we were at his third birthday party. All of Andrew's friends happily ate one piece of cake and then got up to play; Andrew, on the other hand, stayed at the table and just kept eating more and more cake, showing no self-control or internal monitoring. Family members at the party didn't understand our concern. They thought it was normal childhood behaviour and that we were being overly vigilant. The memory of that day still turns my stomach.

The following year, Andrew and David had a major breakthrough. They drove together to our family cottage in the Laurentians in Quebec, and the long drive gave them a chance to bond. From that time on, the two of them developed a close, loving relationship. It was such a relief for me, not only because it gave me a break but because I knew how important it was for David to be close to Andrew. I loved seeing them together.

Throughout this period, Andrew developed seemingly constant ear infections. They had started when he was fourteen months old, and he underwent multiple operations over the next five years to insert tubes into his ears. While they are fairly common among young children, I have since learned that many developmentally disabled children exhibit earlier onset and more frequent ear infections than other children.

As I look back to this time, I have a lot of empathy for the new, inexperienced parents that we were. Although we read a multitude of baby books, we lacked any real knowledge of normal infant/

baby development. We trusted our pediatrician, and we relied on him to guide us. But most pediatricians and other non-specialist professionals are not trained to handle complex mental health concerns. I understand that it can be tricky: they see hundreds of babies and are accustomed to dealing with anxiety-ridden parents who can be needlessly concerned about the littlest sign. That said, I also know that parents should trust their instincts. We strongly suspected that Andrew's behaviour was not normal. Perhaps nothing could have been done or outcomes changed back then, but an acknowledgement and understanding of our concerns could have led to appropriate referrals and earlier intervention by qualified professionals, perhaps changing the course of Andrew's life. I wish that I had taken my own advice and trusted my gut.

RITUALS AND RAGES

As Andrew started nursery school, his teachers suggested that we send him to speech therapy to address his noticeable lisp and slurring. We hadn't realized that his speech was not age appropriate, believing that the lisp was cute at his age and that he would outgrow it.

We found a speech therapist nearby who worked with Andrew weekly over the next two years. Andrew diligently did his speech homework every day with me. Unfortunately, he made little progress, and his lisp, slurring, and rapid and overly loud speech did not improve.

During those sessions, the speech therapist noticed Andrew's hyperactivity and distractibility. She was the first person to mention the possibility that Andrew might have attention deficit disorder (ADD). We were relieved to learn that a professional working with children validated our concerns that something might indeed be wrong.

But in many ways, Andrew was just like other children. He looked forward to nursery school every day and to Gymboree on Saturday mornings with David. We received nothing but glowing reports from his school. He loved being read to, particularly Curious George and the British Fireman Sam series. By the time he entered junior kindergarten, he had lots of friends and couldn't wait to go to school each morning. He believed in following the rules and never got into trouble. He did well academically although his teacher noted his non-stop activity. He brought me much happiness in this period, and I was proud and relieved, thinking naively that our worries might be behind us.

Andrew's early years in grade school continued successfully. He learned to read as expected and enjoyed learning to write and do arithmetic. His teachers described him as a keen and enthusiastic student who was eager to please, even though he needed reminders to stay on task. He remained difficult to understand, and we had to constantly ask him to slow down and repeat. I marvelled at how patient he was with the listener, cheerfully complying and repeating what he had said three, four, and five times in a row.

Andrew and my mother spoke on the phone every day. They seemed to implicitly understand one another and had a special relationship. My mother realized that Andrew had a strong need to connect with others and talk, and she gave him the freedom to do so. She always let him know how much she loved him, covered him in hugs and kisses whenever she saw him, and told him how special he was and how proud she was of him. She told him funny stories that he adored, like the time she met the star baseball player Mickey Mantle at a party without realizing who he was. He returned her love with open arms.

When Andrew was six years old, David and I sought advice from a child psychologist about his continuing food obsession. We met with the psychologist for several months, both together and alone, and he observed both Andrew and Ainsley. His advice — which dismays me now looking back — was that we were being overly vigilant and that we should relax and buy the children a toy kitchen set. He also questioned whether I should continue working full-time in a high-pressure job. I couldn't believe or accept this advice, and we stopped our sessions with him.

In Grade 2, Andrew developed eye tics. They were especially visible during his school's December holiday concert, where he stood in the top row of his class's choir and blinked his eyes repeatedly. They disappeared shortly thereafter, and our doctor chalked them up to a bit of holiday excitement and stress. Andrew continued to love to read books and write stories, as well as to play with his school friends and sister. That year, he also developed a love of baseball that continues to this day. He started closely following the Toronto Blue Jays, and David took him to games at the SkyDome. While not athletic, he did well in baseball, particularly as a catcher, and he even attended baseball day camp that summer.

Andrew's teachers continued to note his chattiness, high activity level, and need for reminders to focus and follow instructions. He also had fine motor difficulties holding a pencil and with his handwriting. As a follow-up to the speech therapist's comment about potential ADD, we spoke with his pediatrician and teacher, but neither believed that he needed any intervention as he was doing so well.

These opinions were nothing new for us. It was tiresome to be constantly told to stop worrying and calm down. We were conflicted about whether to follow our intuitions as new parents or the doctor's "expert" advice and didn't know what to do.

When Andrew was in Grade 3, his teacher again commented on his high activity level and distractibility, and David and I knew that we had to take some action. We pushed our pediatrician to put Andrew on a small Ritalin trial. After a short period, we observed no changes so we stopped the trial. Looking back, I realize that while our doctor was a lovely man, he was not qualified to oversee the trial or determine if Ritalin was the right medication for Andrew, how to titrate dosages, or what type of behaviour therapy to pair with the medication. I wish that we had been lucky enough to work with someone who did have this knowledge and experience so that the trial could have been conducted properly and Andrew could have potentially benefited.

Andrew also started working with an occupational therapist who tried to help him with his fine motor skills, but he made little progress.

My head was spinning with increasing concern as other cracks started to appear that year. We caught Andrew stealing money from us to buy large quantities of candy for his friends and found out that he had been doing so for months. He told us he had done it in order to keep his friends. I was shocked that my innocent little boy would do such a thing.

In spite of these issues, our lives were generally calm. Among my happiest memories during this period was our neighbourhood. Our street was a haven for the children and a fantastic community. Andrew's best friend lived nearby, and the boys spent hours together and slept over at each other's houses. They were inseparable. Our backyard was big enough for a small baseball diamond in the summer and an ice rink in the winter. David and several other neighbourhood fathers spent hours setting up and maintaining the rink, getting up at 5:30 each morning to hose and monitor it. We put up lights and found a glow-in-the-dark puck, and the neighbourhood children and adults enjoyed the rink for years. One of our next-door neighbours had a huge climbing frame and tree house in their backyard; we installed a gate in the fence between our houses so that the children could safely roam between them. And our other next-door neighbour had a pool, so fifteen to twenty children would play together in this idyllic setting. That summer, the children even held a mock wedding for two five-year-olds, inviting all the parents as guests.

Neighbourhood mothers took turns gathering the children for holiday activities. One mother fed the gang dinner and painted their faces before Halloween trick-or-treating. Another was in charge of Easter egg colouring. I took Christmas: I recorded Christmas carols on our piano, practised with the children, and went door to door one evening each year, singing one carol at each house. Depending on how cold it was, more houses were included. We always ended at the retirement home on the next block, where we sang several songs to the residents.

And each summer, about eight of the neighbourhood fathers took the kids camping on Father's Day weekend, while we mothers got to relax and have dinner together. Those weekends were cherished by the children. But David increasingly noted the contrast between Andrew and the other children in their emotional functioning and maturity. Andrew couldn't sit still and demanded more of David's time than Ainsley or the other children asked of their fathers. He had difficulty transitioning between activities, whether playing cops and robbers or capture the flag. David was stymied about why he was so resistant to change.

The year Andrew turned nine, we spent our annual two-week summer vacation at David's family cottage in the Laurentians. The first few days there were filled with swimming, playing tennis, walking through the woods, and enjoying being with David's mother, sister, and her husband.

On the fourth morning, however, seemingly out of nowhere, we witnessed Andrew's first full-blown rage. He stormed out of the living room, went upstairs, and screamed, "I just want to die." The screaming continued for hours. And these rages repeated themselves almost every day. He'd be helping David clear the woods or riding his grandmother's lawn tractor one minute, then start blood-curdling screams the next. He told us that he felt he was going crazy and couldn't identify any reason for these outbursts.

We were terrified. We had no idea what to do, and I woke up each morning full of trepidation about the day to come. We knew that we had to find answers as quickly as possible. We tried everything from coddling Andrew to giving him time-outs, firmer punishments, and crisis intervention–type "hugs." Nothing worked. David's mother was equally perplexed and horrified but didn't want to interfere and largely kept her feelings to herself. I was so thankful to her for tolerating us and not asking us to leave.

Right after we returned home, David and a group of his university friends took their children on another camping trip. David was hesitant to go, given Andrew's rages, and thought about cancelling. But both Andrew and Ainsley were eager to be with their friends, and David did not want to deny them. He hoped that the rages were just temporary.

The trip only served to highlight the increasingly stark differences between Andrew and the other children. Transition times continued to be particularly troublesome. Andrew became overwhelmingly upset and had a tantrum whenever a new activity was planned, whether paddling down the river or playing hide-and-seek. At bedtime, the other children went into their tents to sleep, but Andrew wanted to stay with the adults at the campfire. When he was denied, he threw a fit. David did his best to isolate him from the other children when he became upset and try to calm him down. He worried that Ainsley, who was also on the trip, did not receive as much attention as her brother and was short-changed. Fortunately, she had many good friends in the group and was never lonely.

Within a matter of days after they returned, Andrew started engaging in rituals non-stop. They ranged from him having to touch the floor a set number of times to flicking a light switch on and off 14 times to taking 20 minutes to put on his socks because they didn't feel right. He couldn't walk through doors without going back and forth, sometimes for well over 30 minutes. He had to reread sentences aloud eight times. He repeatedly touched other people's shoulders and engaged in repetitive tapping. He put his teeth on poles and car tires and mirrors, rubbed his head against shrubs, barked and tried to gnaw doors. The rituals quickly mushroomed, all within a matter of a month. It was as if they had been bottled up inside him and came spewing out. His behaviour was so bizarre and shocked us, and I spent all my energy just trying to get through each day.

Then the rituals escalated. Andrew got down on all fours on the subway and licked the filthy floor. He brought home garbage and glass shards and hoarded them under his bed. He put knives in his mouth in order to "feel them." Can you imagine the horror of watching your child place a sharp knife in his mouth? At school, he peeled all the paint off the main hallway outside his classroom. If he woke up in the middle of the night to go to the bathroom, he continued to engage in rituals, tapping my shoulder fourteen times, even though he was half asleep. The rituals seemed to change weekly. He knew that they made no sense but he couldn't stop and they took over his life. He was in deep emotional pain and kept pleading to be "normal" again. I desperately wanted to make his pain disappear.

By this time, I knew that we had to move beyond our pediatrician and find a qualified psychiatrist. The large majority of general practitioners undoubtedly have their patients' best interests in mind and can perhaps handle relatively mild, straightforward cases of ADD or anxiety, but I knew that we needed someone who had experience with the behaviours that Andrew was displaying. It was such a relief to make this decision. We were not afraid of what we might learn; what was important was to find the right help, determine what was wrong with Andrew and what could be done to ameliorate the situation.

THE FIRST DIAGNOSIS

We were fortunate that Andrew's symptoms were so severe that our pediatrician immediately referred us to Dr. Katharina Manassis, a psychiatrist specializing in obsessive-compulsive disorder (OCD) and anxiety disorders at the Hospital for Sick Children in Toronto.

Often, families with less severe symptomology are not so lucky. Many face years of misdiagnoses and are prescribed the wrong medications. They continually search for the correct diagnoses. This is because many of the symptoms in neurodevelopmental disorders can appear similar to one another and can have different causes. We have all heard nightmare stories of children being institutionalized or called intellectually disabled until the truth comes out years later, with great harm done to the child. I understand that many parents don't want to have their child labelled, but the right diagnosis directly correlates with the right treatment plan.

There are no medical or blood tests used to diagnose people with OCD. Instead, doctors observe thoughts and behaviours. We completed a myriad of questionnaires. We learned that while OCD can start at any time, it usually begins before adulthood.

I remember Andrew engaging in rituals in the doctor's waiting room, repeatedly sweeping the floor with his hands.

Dr. Manassis quickly diagnosed Andrew with OCD. She asked if he had had strep infections as a child, since there is a school of thought that some children experience a sudden onset of OCD caused by strep (these are known as PANDAS — pediatric auto-immune neuropsychiatric disorders associated with streptococcal infections). We told her he had had many ear infections but did not believe that he had had strep. She asked Andrew to give his OCD a name (he chose Howie) to try to separate himself from his disorder. And she started him on 50 mg of Luvox, a selective serotonin reuptake inhibitor (SSRI) anti-depressant often used for OCD that changes the brain circuits and chemistry.

We started reading every book we could find about OCD, particularly Judith Rapoport's *The Boy Who Couldn't Stop Washing*, and we watched videos like the International OCD Foundation's *The Touching Tree*. Andrew seemed to have a textbook case of this mental health disorder, which is characterized by unwanted, intrusive thoughts and ideas (*obsessions*) that drive the person to engage in repetitive behaviours and rituals (*compulsions*) in an attempt to get rid of the disturbing thoughts. Compulsions can include washing one's hands for hours until they are raw and bleeding driven by an obsessive fear of germs; counting, tapping, or touching objects a set number of times to ward off the fear of being responsible for hurting someone; and hoarding. Activities like walking through a door or putting on clothes must be repeated until they "feel right." Some people grapple with unwanted sexual or religious thoughts (e.g., fear of offending God). Unfortunately, the compulsions relieve the disturbing thoughts for only a brief period. It's a mystifying disorder that consumes lives.

Thankfully, after three months of adjustments and titrations, the Luvox started to work! Andrew's urges to perform rituals still remained strong but it was such a relief to watch them no longer consume every minute of his life. We — and he — began to have hope.

But the picture wasn't all rosy. There are often side effects and complications with medications, and Luvox was no different. It put Andrew in such a deep sleep that he started wetting his bed every night. Whatever precious sleep and refuge we had was cut short. We had to get up and change his sheets nightly, sometimes twice a night. A waterproof mattress pad didn't help. This continued every night for nine months. Our exhaustion deepened.

Still, the Luvox provided enough relief that we were able to turn our attention to therapy. Therapy is just as important in treating OCD as medication. It gives individuals the strategies and tools they need to deal with their disturbing thoughts and resist engaging in rituals and compulsions. Through Dr. Manassis, I was delighted to find Dr. Jeff Sherman, a clinical behavioural psychologist who specializes in OCD.

Dr. Sherman had a quirky, casual demeanour that put his clients at ease. He wore leather jackets and jeans and enjoyed everything from teaching skiing and taking ballet lessons to avidly watching sports. He and Andrew connected immediately through their shared love of sports.

Dr. Sherman practised a type of cognitive behaviour therapy called exposure and response prevention that is often effective with OCD. The treatment involves slowly *exposing* the OCD sufferer to their fears and helping them to learn not to *respond* to the overwhelming urge to perform a compulsive ritual and let the obsessive thought pass.

Andrew was irrationally fearful of germs and would wash his hands for hours and take multiple long showers every day to relieve his distress. Dr. Sherman had him stand far away from a small pile of dirt and taught him visualization and other techniques that allowed him to move closer and closer to the dirt without having to engage in compulsive, repetitive rituals. It took several weeks, but Andrew was eventually able to place the dirt on his hands for a few seconds ... and then gradually longer. He learned that while he couldn't get rid of or control his disturbing thoughts, he could reduce his distress by letting those fears "wash over him" and not respond to them. He slowly learned to control the disorder.

Andrew wasn't the only person involved in his treatment. As a family, we had to learn not to enable his compulsive rituals. Enablement is a major issue that blocks OCD treatment progress. It could be very frustrating, for example, when we had to get to an appointment but he was stuck turning a light switch on and off for twenty minutes or it took him thirty minutes to put on his socks because they didn't feel right. One afternoon, we were going to meet friends but he couldn't walk through our back door because he had an irrational fear that someone was waiting outside to hurt him. His brain told him to slowly count to twenty-one twelve times in order to relieve the obsession. It would have been so much easier to push him through the door and hurry him up. I wanted to scream at him. Instead, we called our friends and met them forty-five minutes late.

Ainsley was seven at that time, and even at that young age, she played a major role helping Andrew. She learned not to enable his rituals and would encourage him and root him on. He turned to her for comfort. I remember many an evening when they crawled into bed together and she put her arms around him and soothed him.

During this period, Andrew constantly asked for reassurance. Dr. Sherman led us through sessions that taught us how best to help Andrew. While giving in and providing that reassurance would have given him temporary relief and allowed us to get on with our lives, it would have done nothing to lessen his OCD. It would have been easy to avoid activities that triggered his OCD, such as taking a longer route home to avoid something he feared on the way. But we knew that it was critical not to enable him. It was okay if we were late or missed an appointment. We learned effective visualization techniques, like helping him place an unwanted thought in a pretend balloon and watch the balloon slowly float away. His anxiety lessened the further away the balloon flew.

It was such a joy to see Andrew learning to control his OCD and managing better. We talked openly with one another about the challenges that he was facing and celebrated his progress. Ainsley made him a paper crown, told him how proud she was of him, and hugged him often. We weren't out of the woods, by any means, but we knew that we were on the right track.

THE RAGES CONTINUE

Though Andrew was learning to control his OCD, daily life remained harsh. For the next eight months, his rages continued at home unabated, often for hours at a time. He was able to hold it together at school, but once he was home where he felt safe, he exploded. As we later learned, this is not uncommon. He was miserable and hated the rages but couldn't stop.

I felt numb, operating on autopilot. While it was a relief to watch his OCD recede, I knew that Andrew was suffering from additional complexities. David and I understood that we had to keep looking for answers, and I ploughed ahead with research and calls to a myriad of medical professionals.

To help cope with the rages, we emptied the children's playroom of all furniture and brought in huge throw pillows to protect Andrew and us and allow him to vent. He was still small enough to be carried down to the playroom when the rages started, and he hadn't been violent or hurt any of us yet, but I was fearful that would change. The day Andrew's rage drove Ainsley out into the snow in her nightgown was the day that I really started to worry about what we would do as Andrew grew bigger.

David kept telling me not to worry, that we would eventually find solutions, but at times it seemed futile. Andrew punched holes in walls, ranted, and swore at anyone and anything in his way.

David vividly remembers the four of us coming home with another family after an outing to a park one afternoon and having to wrestle Andrew to the ground when he started raging for no apparent reason. He became a child we didn't recognize, crying out, swearing, and kicking non-stop. David carried him into the playroom and held the door closed while Andrew screamed; our friends were shocked, particularly at David having to hold the door shut. They tried to be polite and stayed for a while but understandably made their exit as quickly as they could.

I will forever be indebted to the children's British nanny, who stayed with us throughout this period and supported us. She had joined our family shortly after Ainsley was born, long before we knew that either child would face serious mental health issues. She cared for the children deeply and learned alongside us. She essentially became a member of our family, and her parents visited almost every summer and stayed with us. We were so fortunate she understood that Andrew was not at fault, that we were desperately doing our best, and that we needed her. I remember eating an entire pint of coffee Häagen-Dazs ice cream with her one afternoon as we waited out one rage.

Over time, we learned how to gauge when a rage was over. Andrew's screams would slowly turn to crying, and we would go down and hold him. This gentle, loving boy sobbed that the behaviour wasn't him, that he was deeply unhappy, and that he wanted and needed treatment. While heartbreaking, this made me even more determined to find the right diagnoses and treatments.

The constant rages meant that David and I had to stop socializing with friends, and Ainsley couldn't bring her friends over. We never knew when a rage would start and didn't want to risk shocking or alienating anyone. With no family in Toronto, we struggled to find a babysitter who could handle the children when our nanny wasn't working. After Andrew locked one babysitter out of the house, the agency told us never to call again. I was bereft and felt increasingly lonely and isolated.

On top of everything else that Andrew endured that year, he lost a close school friend. The boys had a minor physical altercation one day but quickly recovered and started playing together again regularly. A few weeks later, however, his friend suddenly stopped coming over or inviting Andrew to his house. We considered his parents friends, so we had a hard time coming to terms with the sudden loss of contact. It felt cruel and ignorant. Instead of giving us the support that we desperately needed in this vulnerable time, they pulled their son away, claiming that he had become overly dependent on Andrew. We tried to talk to them, but they had no interest in hearing us out. Andrew was devastated. David and I couldn't believe that the parents would hurt Andrew so deeply.

Fortunately, twin boys in Andrew's class who had moved to Toronto from Germany, as well as another classmate who lived down the street, were understanding and stuck by him. The twins' parents also showed David and me great friendship and caring. I remember weeping at their house one evening while the wife quietly comforted and held me. Sadly, they were the exception. Most families either did not understand or were too scared to engage. People simply vanished from our lives.

Thankfully, in spite of all his challenges and differences, Andrew was never teased by his peers. Ainsley was so protective of Andrew, and she undoubtedly would have beaten them up if they had! Perhaps Andrew escaped this treatment because he was so friendly and likeable. Whatever the reasons, it was a relief that he didn't have to deal with teasing and bullying as an added stressor.

DIAGNOSTIC PROGRESS

———

In Grade 4, Andrew's teacher became one of our angels. Nora McKay was highly regarded, known for caring for all her students, communicating with the parents, and taking the bigger picture into perspective, not solely focusing on academics.

She noted Andrew's increasing academic difficulties and strongly believed that these challenges extended beyond the intrusiveness of his OCD. Although he had had no difficulty learning to read, write, or do simple mathematics, his difficulty transitioning between activities continued and he lacked abstract thinking capabilities. He completed assignments too quickly and carelessly and was distractible. He needed learning strategies to help him focus, plan, and organize his work.

Ms. McKay was the most empathetic teacher Andrew could have had. She understood what he and we were experiencing, gave him attention and understanding, and supported him the best she could. She kept him back when the rest of the class attended French lessons, recognizing that French was far beyond his capabilities. She cut back on his homework. She communicated with David and me daily and worked closely with us, both at school and at home. There were days when I could hardly function, and she sent me off to work, understanding that my job was my refuge.

Andrew's physical appearance also increasingly differed from his peers: his head hung down and his eyes were shaded and peeked out. His speech was often unintelligible, his mouth hung open, he drooled, and he had poor posture.

He also engaged in repetitive body movements to help calm himself, self-stimulating behaviour known as "stimming" that is common in children and adults with autism. He massaged his shoulders and rubbed the top of his head repeatedly. He displayed physical tics, such as repetitive eye blinking, throwing his neck back, or picking his scabs, and vocal tics, such as humming, coughing, or clearing his throat for weeks at a time. The constant throat clearing, in particular, drove me up a wall.

One day, we were walking our dog in a nearby park and Andrew was vocally ticking, making repetitive noises that sounded like hooting. As we walked down a path by a river, a passerby came up to Andrew and asked if he was okay. I was accustomed to New Yorkers sometimes being as forward as this, but not Canadians, and I feared that Andrew would be upset. Without missing a beat, however, he looked her straight in the eye and responded that he was bird calling. I burst out laughing.

By this time, we suspected that Andrew had Tourette syndrome, a neurological disorder characterized by physical and vocal tics that are extremely difficult to control. Tourette syndrome has been sensationalized in the media, often portrayed as uncontrolled, non-stop swearing outbursts (called coprolalia). In reality, only a small minority of people with Tourette have coprolalia.

We also suspected that he had ADD and learning disabilities. We found a support group for parents of children with ADD, and our first session confirmed our suspicions. It was exciting to find a community of parents who were experiencing many of the same symptoms and behaviours we were undergoing. But we were stymied to learn that none of their children had rages. We knew that something didn't fit.

Andrew's challenges led us to undergo the Identification, Placement, and Review Committee (IPRC) process with Ms. McKay, Andrew's principal, and the Ontario Ministry of Education in the winter of Grade 4. This process determines whether a student can be classified as "exceptional" and receive special education assistance. As part of the process, Andrew completed an independent psychoeducational assessment, which concluded that his challenges warranted placing him in special education. In addition to his difficulties sustaining attention and controlling his impulses to move and talk, his anxiety and worried thoughts interfered with his concentration, exacerbated by his compulsive rituals. Increasingly serious grapho-motor problems — the physical ability to write — were evidenced, with clear coordination issues. He also had difficulty with more complex, abstract concepts. After meeting with the committee, Andrew was deemed "exceptional," to be placed in special education when available. This process taught me how critical it is for any special-needs child in the public school system to undergo this process, as it is the only way to obtain the specialized resources needed.

I was pleased that Andrew would be able to move into the special education program, but David and I felt that he might need more specialized help. He was almost eleven years old that spring, and we decided to proactively look for a small, structured school for special-needs children. We found the Douglas Academy, a small private grade school headed by a woman named Colleen Bacon that catered to children like Andrew. Class sizes averaged four students. Andrew immediately fell in love with Colleen and her caring staff. Colleen was short in stature but a firecracker of a woman. She had sparkly eyes, an infectious laugh, loved each of her students, and had an upbeat, "can do" attitude. The school was perfect for him, and Colleen informed Andrew that he could start immediately. He happily transferred there in April of that school year.

While I was delighted that we had found a good match for him, I couldn't help but think back to the discussions that David and I had had when I was pregnant about which private schools he should attend. Andrew's special needs made us realize how ludicrous these concerns were in hindsight. Who cared if he went to an elite private school? Who cared if he got into University of Toronto or Harvard? We stopped thinking about his future and instead focused our energy on supporting him to get through each day and function to the best of his abilities.

Colleen quickly referred us to Dr. Till Davy, a developmental pediatrician with a special interest in and gift for working with special-needs children. Dr. Davy reminded me of the psycho-analyst Sigmund Freud: he spoke with an Austrian accent and sported a beard. And he had a wicked sense of humour that I adored. During the initial visit, he spent over an hour with David and me, carefully listening to us, letting us know that we were not alone and confirming that we knew our child better than any medical professional. He then spent one hour sitting on the floor with Andrew. The connection between them was immediate, and Dr. Davy's empathy and understanding still bring tears to my eyes. Watching Andrew hug him repeatedly and seeing him look forward to each visit filled me with joy. I had never before inter-acted with a medical professional who was both able to empathize with and understand us while at the same time able to relate to a child on his level. Dr. Davy became one of our angels.

Dr. Davy prescribed 0.5 mg of the anti-psychotic medication Risperdal, which stopped Andrew's rages within two days. We could hardly believe it. He also prescribed desmopressin, a simple nasal spray sold under the name DDAVP that stopped Andrew's nightly bed wetting. Andrew was overjoyed. I was ecstatic with these changes, although I kicked myself that we hadn't found Dr. Davy earlier.

Meanwhile, Dr. Manassis informed us that due to the number of disorders Andrew had and the delicate interaction between the medications prescribed to treat them, we should seek out physicians in the United States. The doctors there benefited from seeing more children like Andrew due to the country's much larger population. Dr. Davy agreed; while he had a great interest in developmental disabilities, OCD, and ADD, he was not a specialist and he wanted to ensure that we had access to the greatest expertise and latest thinking in psychiatry.

I called ten leading hospitals east of the Mississippi to obtain their advice about whom to see, and the name Dr. Joseph Biederman kept coming up. Dr. Biederman is a world-renowned neuropsychopharmacologist at Massachusetts General Hospital in Boston with deep clinical, scientific, and research expertise. I called and after just five months of waiting (many families wait far longer to see specialists), we were able to get an appointment.

Dr. Biederman became another one of our angels. I found his soft-spoken, non-judgmental, open, and accessible demeanour truly unusual. He was totally client-focused. He was so warm and empathetic that Andrew immediately embraced him. And we all laughed because, even at that age, Andrew was almost as tall as Dr. Biederman was short.

Dr. Biederman and his team spent three days testing and observing Andrew. He confirmed Andrew's diagnoses of Tourette syndrome, OCD, ADD, short-cycle bipolar disorder, and learning disabilities. He told us that many people with Tourette syndrome suffer from rages. Tourette syndrome tends to act as the "umbrella" diagnosis, and many people with Tourette also have OCD and ADD. Dr. Biederman adjusted or increased a number of Andrew's medications, and we hoped that our son would stabilize. I was overjoyed that Andrew was in Dr. Biederman's hands and felt some hope and even cautious optimism emerge inside me. Andrew was equally thrilled to know that his disorders could be addressed and better controlled under Dr. Biederman's care.

Unfortunately, the changing dosages and new medications played havoc with each other. The anti-psychotic medication Risperdal and the ADD medication Concerta had opposing side effects. Risperdal caused Andrew to gain three pounds a week (this is not uncommon). His ADD medications, on the other hand, tended to suppress his appetite and sleep. Although Andrew seemed unperturbed by these changes, I was scared and acutely aware of the side effects. But Dr. Biederman advised us that these reactions were not unusual and that they would settle over time. And sure enough, Andrew's rapid weight gain stopped after six weeks.

None of these medications had such severe side effects that we stopped them, but neuropsychopharmacology is clearly an art, not just a science. Dr. Biederman carefully monitored the effects and interactions of the medications to determine the optimal suite of medications for Andrew. Andrew's confidence grew as he started to gain more control of his behaviour, and I found myself beginning to relax for the first time in a year.

A NUGGET OF HOPE

From then on, Andrew and I travelled to Boston twice a year to see Dr. Biederman, and we were in touch regularly between visits. I was awed that Dr. Biederman responded to any emails and calls I placed to him almost immediately, even on weekends and evenings, because he was in such high demand with patients, his colleagues, and international conferences and meetings.

Dr. Biederman introduced medication changes and increases multiple times, especially the Risperdal, over the next several years. We continually monitored the interactions between the medications and their side effects. Dr. Davy suggested that Andrew try eye movement desensitization and reprocessing (EMDR), a treatment that encourages individuals to focus on an unwanted thought or memory with repetitive eye movements to stimulate the brain's processing system. We were open to trying new approaches and trialled this treatment for three months but it did not work for Andrew.

During one of our early meetings with Dr. Biederman, he suggested we get a therapy dog for Andrew. I was skeptical and wondered how we would ever be able to take care of a dog on top of our family challenges. David had grown up with dogs, however, and was confident. I called the local Lions Club, and they put us on their waitlist for dogs that had been rejected from their dog guide program due to temperament or health. Shortly thereafter, we brought home a one-year-old golden retriever who had been rejected due to cataracts. We named her Nugget after the colour of her coat. To my amusement, most of the children on the block thought that we had named her after McDonald's chicken nuggets. Nugget was patient and loving. David bemoaned the fact that she didn't really play or chase balls like many dogs, but she would calmly wait whenever Andrew was upset and then cover him with licks. He loved holding her, and she helped calm him down.

We also wanted Andrew to have a Canadian psychiatrist as a local resource and backup to Dr. Biederman. He started seeing Dr. Paul Sandor, the head psychiatrist at Toronto's leading Tourette syndrome neurodevelopmental clinic, once a year. Dr. Sandor is one of the kindest, gentlest, and most understanding medical professionals that I know, looking on with patience and amusement as Andrew tried to probe his personal life with glee. Upon learning that Dr. Sandor was born in Eastern Europe, for example, he asked him whether he had been a spy. Dr. Sandor agreed with the medications and dosages that Dr. Biederman had prescribed.

Dr. Sherman also continued to work with Andrew and expanded the scope of his therapy beyond exposure and response prevention to cognitive behaviour therapy, a structured type of therapy that helps clients learn how to better understand and deal with their problems.

Dr. Sherman recognized that Andrew could not sit still in an office, so he came to the house and took him on long walks and out for meals. To help Andrew learn to control his impulsivity, he took him to a Nike store — at the time one of Andrew's favourite brands — and let him try on shoes that he wanted, then taught him to let the urgent desire to buy them pass. He instituted an incentive system in which Andrew earned points towards baseball memorabilia whenever he lied about something and was able to admit to us that he had lied rather than hiding it. Andrew responded to this personal approach and developed a trusted relationship with Dr. Sherman.

After each session, Dr. Sherman debriefed with David and me. We worked together to develop action plans, with additional behavioural contracts and incentives. And we kept each other informed about Andrew's behaviours. Andrew sometimes tried to manipulate us to get what he wanted by claiming that Dr. Sherman supported something we had refused. Or he would tell Dr. Sherman the same thing about us. It didn't take us long to figure out what he was doing, and the three of us stayed in close touch to ensure that we were on the same page.

It was through these experiences that I learned the importance of working in a coordinated manner with all of Andrew's caregivers, from his nanny and teachers to his health care professionals. It was critical to tell his teacher if he had had a rough night, whether he had struggled to complete his homework, had had a two-hour rage and was exhausted, was ticking by throwing his neck back so often that he was in pain, or was upset because he had hurt Ainsley or had lied. Similarly, his teachers let me know how his day had gone each afternoon. Andrew was an open book who brought everything that happened at home into the classroom and vice versa; his heightened anxiety meant that unless he had closure of a situation that upset him, he couldn't function in any environment. Dr. Sherman and Andrew's teachers worked together on strategies, like instituting more breaks and chunking his tasks into smaller, more manageable pieces. Dr. Sherman always wrote to Dr. Biederman before we went to Boston to add his perspective to our input. For example, after hearing from Dr. Sherman and from us about Andrew's ongoing mood swings and increasing anxiety, Dr. Biederman increased Andrew's dosage of Risperdal to 2 mg twice a day and of Luvox to 100 mg twice a day to further help control these challenges.

Equally important for Andrew was bringing a pet into our home who provided a calm and soothing presence and who essentially acted as an additional caregiver. As a team, all his caregivers brought Andrew and our family hope for the future, cementing in me the strong belief that it is only by partnering in a clear and transparent manner that a special-needs child's challenges can be optimally addressed. This is one of the mantras that I live by.

FINDING THE RIGHT FIT

———

Andrew's evolving coordinated care approach not only had positive effects on his life but benefited his learning. By now, he was in Grade 5, and his teachers consistently described him as enthusiastic, cooperative, considerate, and conscientious, with a positive attitude. He loved interacting with his peers but was most comfortable with Colleen and the teachers, whom he would hug every morning. His sense of humour was evident, and he learned to manage his grapho-motor problems by using a keyboard; in fact, he became so proficient on the computer that he even tutored some students when he was in Grade 8.

His impulsivity and distractibility, however, remained difficult to contain. He rushed through his work, talked too much, too quickly, and too loudly. He had inconsistent listening skills. Periods of transition and change continued to be particularly challenging for him. He required regular reassurances that he was on track. His confusion with new concepts, particularly those that were abstract or had inferences, became more evident as he progressed though middle school. Expressions like "comparing apples to oranges" or "killing two birds with one stone" eluded him. Math word problems confused him. And he became easily overwhelmed and anxious in group activities like physical education and recess due to the competitive, more aggressive nature of sports. Baseball continued to be the ongoing exception.

As he matured, Andrew became very self-aware of his strengths and areas of development. He was able to explain what he was experiencing and started to advocate for himself.

Andrew thrived under Colleen's and his teachers' understanding guidance. He made good friends and loved going to school. The school made it clear that we were not to help with homework, which provided more respite for me. And the caring extended beyond 9 a.m. to 3 p.m.: teachers and staff sent daily notes and calls home that provided important feedback about Andrew's day, and we shared back how Andrew's evening or weekend had been. Colleen called with advice and observations about the need for potential medication and therapy changes, and she met with Dr. Sherman and us on many occasions so that we could work together. School was a safe place and a haven for Andrew and for us.

Through the school, we connected with several families who became good friends. One of Andrew's best friends at Douglas was a tall, lanky, mischievous boy named Duncan. Although both boys shared diagnoses of ADD and OCD, Duncan could not have been more different than Andrew. Duncan was a risk taker, while Andrew was risk averse. Duncan was largely irresponsible at home and in school, only begrudgingly completing his homework, while Andrew had no such issues. And Duncan didn't care about rules, while Andrew was rule-bound. Yet they enjoyed each other's friendship, and we became friends with the entire family. I fondly remember joint family dinners: the meals themselves were pure chaos and finished within twenty minutes, with the kids running around wildly. But the fact that we didn't have to worry about shocking or offending each other was a huge relief. It felt like a sitcom, filled with laughter and happiness — the first time we had experienced this with others in years. It was so meaningful to have dinners that we could not have with "normal" families, who would have been horrified at the children's behaviour and the rapidity of our meals, with no lingering for conversation. Duncan's mother and I understood each other and the challenges we faced, and we regularly turned to each other for support.

It was during this period, when Andrew was almost eleven years old, that he went away for the summer for the first time. Through Dr. Biederman, I found Summit Camp in Pennsylvania, an overnight camp for hundreds of children with ADD. Andrew had previously attended a variety of day camps, but it was increasingly difficult for them to understand and accommodate his needs. Summit was geared to youth with social and emotional learning challenges and hired experienced staff trained in working with children with these issues.

Andrew signed up to attend Summit for four weeks, but after two weeks there, he called and pleaded with us to stay the full eight-week session. We were delighted and a bit shocked! He was never homesick and was at peace at Summit, where similar children and happiness surrounded him. He participated in all the activities from swimming to singalongs and particularly enjoyed bantering with the caring and fun staff. We were thrilled to let him stay, although it took about two weeks for David and me to wind down and start to enjoy the break from him.

As we unwound, the world began to reopen for us. We hired a sitter for Ainsley and went out for dinner, both by ourselves and with friends. One night, while we were out at a pub with Duncan's parents, we laughed until tears ran down our faces as we told stories about our sons. It was only when dessert arrived that we looked around and I realized that we were having more fun than anyone else at the restaurant.

The summer flew by. I started to brace for Andrew's return well before the end of camp. I was proud of how well he had done at Summit and that he'd been able to have a successful time away. I couldn't wait to see him again and hear his stories. But I also mourned the end of this period of respite.

That summer gave me the time to reflect on the importance of having friends we could relate to and the toll that challenges with our families took. Socializing with parents of similar children laid a foundation of trust and understanding between us that allowed us to relax more than with our other friends — and even with family — and put our lives in better perspective and balance. For example, although Andrew's rapid eighteen-pound weight gain from Risperdal was alarming, another boy in his class had gained over seventy pounds on the medication; his parents agreed with us that this miracle medication was worth putting up with its adverse effects.

My mother in New York, on the other hand, stunned me by saying, "Well, you don't want a fat child." The fact that she didn't understand was heartbreaking to me. I felt I had lost my main support. Thankfully, she came around several months later and was horrified at what she had said. She continued to hurt more for me than for Andrew, repeatedly telling me that I didn't deserve what was happening in my life.

David's family was generally careful not to voice their opinions about Andrew's diagnoses and challenges. I don't know if they felt that they shouldn't intrude or that we wouldn't appreciate their views. Perhaps there were other reasons. David and I were partly responsible and shielded them from the full reality of the situation, as he wasn't comfortable exposing our lives to them in greater detail.

These experiences taught me the benefits of spending time with those who could empathize with our struggles. Facing what appeared to be overwhelming obstacles at times, we lacked the reserves and energy to deal with those who didn't truly understand our reality. It was rewarding to socialize with parents undergoing similar challenges. They not only provided needed support and a shoulder to cry on but the opportunity to laugh with us at our seemingly surreal lives.

HIGH SCHOOL APPROACHES

In Andrew's last year at Douglas, a filmmaker who had heard about Andrew through SickKids Hospital contacted us to ask if Andrew and our family would be willing to participate in the National Film Board of Canada documentary *OCD: The War Inside*. The documentary was directed by two seasoned filmmakers, one of whom had OCD himself, and told the poignant stories of four individuals with severe OCD. We agreed. Andrew was thrilled and thought he might even become famous. And David and I were delighted to have the opportunity to better educate the public about OCD.

Through the documentary, the filmmakers gave the audience an inside look at the lives of those fighting to survive "a war inside their minds." They interviewed Andrew extensively about the details of his OCD, the distress it caused him and his medications and treatment. They filmed him in various locales, from our home to the classroom to the baseball mound. They included Ainsley, David, and me, asking us questions about the effects of Andrew's OCD on the family. The four of us were invited to the Toronto premiere, where Andrew and the other participants were feted and received a standing ovation at the conclusion of the film. The documentary won multiple awards, including the Silver Chris Award at the Columbus International Film & Video Festival, the Audience Award at the Rendezvous with Madness Film Festival, and the Jury Prize at Superfest.

As high school approached, I contacted our local public high school, which had a well-known special education program. They quietly advised us that, with funding cuts, our vulnerable son would be placed in the same classroom as oppositional and emotionally disturbed teenagers. I was thankful that they let me know and immediately started to research private school options.

The only local option we found was a small private school just one subway stop away from us. The staff were lovely and caring, but the school lacked the size and resources to be able to offer activities like sports, music, and the arts in addition to academics. We wanted a more rounded experience for Andrew that would expose him to all aspects of high school life, so we crossed it off the list.

Through more research and sourcing, I found the independent boarding school Eagle Hill School in Hardwick, Massachusetts. A pioneer in the special education field, the school adhered to the belief that each student must be understood and supported as an individual with a unique learning profile. It followed a holistic approach, blending academic subjects with courses like physical education, woodshop, and graphic design. The curriculum also focused on social and personal growth. Class sizes were small, averaging six students each, and teachers used multi-sensory strategies targeted to each student's level.

At the time, Eagle Hill served about 125 high school students with ADD and learning disabilities. Although it was far away from our home in Toronto, the location suited us because it was relatively close to Dr. Biederman. We visited several times, met with the headmaster, and fell in love with the structured, highly individualized program and bucolic New England campus. Andrew was enthralled with everything about the school. The headmaster told us that taking Andrew would be an experiment for the school due to his complex profile with multiple disorders, but they were willing to try.

Andrew couldn't wait to start. The only thing that made him sad was how much he was going to miss Ainsley. They were closer than ever and were able to calm each other down better than anyone else when they were in crisis.

While I knew that living apart from Ainsley would be a big adjustment for Andrew, I had no compunction about him spending the academic year in Massachusetts. He had thrived at Summit Camp, and I knew that we would chat with him every day and see him on breaks and visiting days. I also knew that he would have the support of my family: my mother was not too far away in New York, and one of my cousins lived about an hour away.

At Andrew's Grade 8 graduation from Douglas, Colleen arranged for dinner at a local restaurant for the four graduating students and their families. Everyone then returned to our house for dessert and celebrations. Colleen presented each student with the gift of an atlas with a special message for each of them. She wrote that Andrew had taught her a great deal about perseverance and what it means to tackle challenges head on. We were so proud of how far he had come, and it was clear that he felt the same way. He was confident in his future and excited about moving on.

ANDREW THE TEENAGER

Andrew settled into Eagle Hill with ease. He loved everything about the school and told us that it felt like home from the start. He found a community of students facing similar challenges and a caring faculty and staff who treated every student with respect. He enjoyed being able to learn at his own pace in small classes with individualized attention. And he loved the sports program, especially baseball, basketball, and golf.

Academically, Andrew remained an upbeat, enthusiastic student, willing to grow and improve. He particularly enjoyed literature and composition. When his class read *Othello*, his teacher worked one-on-one with him to explain the words, and the class watched the movie and acted out the speeches in current-day English. Math remained extremely difficult for him, but his teachers all willingly gave their time after class, and he would often meet with them for an hour each afternoon. And while Andrew didn't usually enjoy science, he loved his biology class. The teacher made it come alive — for example, teaching the origin of the human species with this acronym that Andrew can still remember almost twenty years later:

Kleenex — for *Kingdom*
Prevents — for *Phylum*
Colds — for *Class*
Often — for *Order*
From — for *Family*
Getting — for *Genus*
Spread — for *Species*

Although Andrew's grades were strong, his deficits became increasingly apparent. Testing in Grade 9 ranked him in the twenty-fifth percentile range for word meaning and mathematics. By the time he reached Grade 12, with the increasing complexity and abstract concepts in the curriculum, the same tests would rank him below average in every academic area, in particular in math, where he was below the tenth percentile. He had reached his academic potential and could make only marginal gains. But there were two non-academic classes where he shone: he excelled in graphic design, an honours course in which he designed a Toronto Blue Jays website. And he did very well in woodshop, where he made our family a beautiful grandfather clock, golf display case, and wooden bench and built my mother a lovely coffee table that she proudly displayed in her den.

Even with his previous weight gain from Risperdal, Andrew was very thin. We joked that he looked like Ichabod Crane, but I was concerned that his then-6'2" frame was dangerously skinny at 128 pounds. The school ensured that he ate healthfully and followed Dr. Biederman's advice to give him two milkshakes a day. He also worked with a psychologist weekly, as well as with a speech therapist (to no avail). The psychologist tried to get him to sit with his head and neck up, as well as to maintain eye contact with others for a sustained time. There was little progress, and I remained particularly concerned that he would experience debilitating neck and back pain in the future from his terrible posture.

Socially, Andrew preferred to spend his free time in his first year with some of his teachers and the school nurse, with whom he became particularly close, rather than hanging out with students his age. He felt more comfortable and safer with adults than with his peers, as he had at Douglas. As his confidence grew, however, his peer interactions improved and he was viewed as a friend to all. He joined several clubs, such as golf and community clean-up, and was very proud to be selected as the scoreboard operator for basketball and wrestling.

These successes earned Andrew the honour of Semi-Independent Status, which gave him no-curfew privileges and a key to the dorm, as well as no mandatory study hall. He recognized that the school's rules provided him with a framework that lessened his anxiety, and he continued to follow them.

I felt that I had also earned the privilege of Semi-Independent Status! With Andrew away during the academic year, we had more breathing room, and I found that life regained some normalcy. We talked with Andrew multiple times each day and communicated with the school regularly, but we didn't have to live minute-to-minute. We were able to go out for dinner, socialize with others, and, most importantly, relax. I was able to read biographies and crime novels and watch funny movies, which I had had to abandon over the past five years. It was liberating.

However, crises continued to occur. Andrew called us in the spring of his first year at Eagle Hill and told us that he was having hallucinations. He was scared. This was shortly after he had joined a class trip to a local movie theatre to see *A Beautiful Mind*, the biographical film based on mathematician John Nash's life that chronicles his struggles with schizophrenia. It took us several weeks, with support from the school and his team of professionals, to realize that the movie had caused him severe anxiety and that he was not really having delusions. Once we identified this, he himself recognized that he had not been hallucinating. His tics increased for a while but eventually subsided.

I did not find it overly difficult to deal with Andrew's crises from a distance. The school was excellent at communicating and partnering with us. And the distance actually gave me room to gain perspective and see the bigger picture rather than becoming caught up and mired in every little issue.

Andrew came home that summer and was able to secure a job as a computer counsellor at a day camp that was five minutes from our house in Toronto. The owners had a family member with Tourette syndrome and were very supportive and understanding, as well as appreciating his capabilities. Andrew enjoyed teaching the campers and was thrilled to earn money for the first time.

Over the next two years, we settled into a familiar rhythm of Andrew coming home each summer and working as a computer counsellor at the camp. And this successful work experience led him to secure a summer job with a company that set up computers for several private grade schools in his last summer before finishing high school.

In his final year at Eagle Hill, at age seventeen, Andrew decided to submit a personal essay to the *Globe & Mail*'s Facts & Arguments page. He increasingly enjoyed advocating and educating others about his disorders and thought that sharing his story could help raise more awareness. He wrote about his OCD and how it didn't define him. He described his diagnoses and treatment to date and how his happy days as a young child had been interrupted by non-stop obsessive thoughts and compulsive rituals, writing, "Above all, it was my will and determination to control this demon that turned my frightening situation into a manageable life." It was published in November 2004 with the title "Seeking Peace in a War with Myself." Seeing his words in print filled Andrew, as well as David, Ainsley, and me, with great pride. He received a huge number of accolades from family members, school friends, neighbours, and many strangers who were touched by what he had written. We framed the article and placed it prominently on a shelf in his bedroom.

COMING HOME

As graduation neared, Andrew underwent a cognitive and educational evaluation, as every graduating student at Eagle Hill did, to help determine his optimal post-secondary placement.

I had always told the children that they could do anything they wanted and be whatever they wanted and that they were not defined by their disabilities. Andrew — with no lack of self-confidence and grandiose ideas — decided that he wanted to go to Massachusetts Institute of Technology. However, the psychologist's report, with which David and I concurred, stated that he was not suited for university and should enrol in a program with a vocational bent. Andrew was furious and vehemently disagreed, ranting on and on about the psychologist misunderstanding his capabilities. It took years for him to come around, and I blamed myself for having allowed him to have such unrealistic dreams that he doesn't have the capability to reach. It was unfair to him, and to this day I continue to feel largely responsible for creating such disappointment and its ensuing anger in him.

Instead of MIT, Eagle Hill introduced Andrew to a life-skills program an hour away where he could attend the local community college and study computer science. He was interested in a technology-oriented career and became excited about attending.

Andrew graduated in June 2005, and it was a momentous occasion. He stood tall in his green cap and gown as he received his diploma and posed for pictures, hugged the faculty and staff, and promised his best friends that they would stay in touch. David and I were extremely proud of the progress that he had made. I thought he might become emotional at the ceremony, but he had already mentally moved on and was focused on enrolling in the life-skills program with his best friend from Eagle Hill.

It quickly became apparent, however, that the program was not the right fit for Andrew. The staff taught life skills that were too basic for him, and the community college had stopped offering computer science courses unbeknownst to us. Both Andrew and we were unhappy that the program had neglected to inform us of this change. After four months there, Andrew packed up his bags with our blessing and moved back to Toronto right before Christmas.

I was delighted to have Andrew home and looked forward to helping him plan his future. To celebrate his return, he and I purchased tickets to a George Carlin concert. George was his favourite comedian, and he listened to his comedy routines for hours. He particularly enjoyed when George dissected language — for example, asking how it's possible to "pre-board" a plane. I marvelled at how Andrew understood the turns of phrases that George cleverly used, given his difficulty understanding abstract, inferential language.

About a month before the concert, I wrote to George's agent to ask if George would shake hands with Andrew when he was in Toronto. The agent arranged for them to meet at intermission. Andrew was over the moon. I explained to him that he would likely be one of many fans lined up to say hello. To my surprise,

Andrew was the only person set to meet him. George brought him into his dressing room and spent the entire intermission with him. Andrew told him that he was a huge fan and that he loved listening to him even though he understood language literally. They discussed everything from comedy to basketball, and Andrew was in awe. He found George to be very calm and mellow, unlike his show business persona. Upon George's return to California, he sent Andrew two books. The kindness of strangers can be breathtaking.

ENTERING THE WORLD OF WORK

—

Andrew was relieved to be back in Toronto and settled into home life fairly easily. He continued therapy with Dr. Sherman and was eager to start his career right away. I was pleased with how motivated he was to find the right job.

Finding meaningful employment can be challenging for many new graduates but is especially so for developmentally disabled individuals, who all too often face uneducated prejudice and discrimination. The fact that they look "different" and have limited intellectual and cognitive abilities make it more difficult for them to follow directions or sustain attention. They can be difficult to understand, and their social skills are often viewed as deficient as they can have difficulty maintaining eye contact or understanding social cueing. There can be unfounded concern that customers and other employees will be scared by them. Any upset at work can lead to heightened stress, and they need more oversight and supervision than many other employees.

Most workplaces do not have systems and processes in place that accommodate these individuals or incorporate customized solutions for them. These accommodations can include writing out work tasks step-by-step, providing checklists, and allowing the employee to work the same hours each day instead of changing shifts. Andrew knew that he would need many of these accommodations to succeed, and I reassured him that I would always advocate on his behalf with his employers.

Andrew wanted a job in the computer field and asked for my assistance job hunting. I helped him apply to the Ontario Disability Support Program (ODSP), a provincial social assistance program that provides employment and income supports to eligible Ontario residents with disabilities. He had to fill out an application and show proof of his disabilities through letters from his doctors, and we attended an in-person interview together. It was a fairly complex process that he could not have completed without assistance. Andrew qualified for employment supports but not income support, as David and I had put away money in both children's names each year from the time they were born.

Through ODSP, Andrew trained with a tutor/mentor and secured two computer certifications. He volunteered as a computer trainer at a hospital, and ODSP provided him with an internship at a company where he learned to repair and upgrade computers for non-profit organizations. He then secured a full-time job with a wholesale distributor of computers and software. He stayed there for almost two years but became unhappy as the company had little interest in accommodating his unique needs and capabilities.

While he was still employed there, Andrew took the initiative to apply to our local grocery store, which was three blocks from our house. He had become interested in customer service and always enjoyed chatting with the cashiers whenever we went food shopping. He was hired on the spot as a cashier. He was unsurprised that he was hired so quickly, fully confident of his abilities. He memorized the produce codes and loved interacting with the customers. He consistently received rave reviews from them as he chatted them up, showing particular interest in their children. He remembered their names and important events in their lives and made them smile. I remember going to the store one day and observing four customers waiting to check out on Andrew's line while three other cashiers had no customers. When staff tried to redirect them to these empty cashier stations, every one of them said that they preferred to wait for Andrew. Tears formed in my eyes: "Wow!" I thought proudly. It was so meaningful for Andrew to find employment where he was valued for his strengths and abilities.

Andrew loved his job and worked happily there for the next two years. Then, one day, we learned that the store's parent company had hired two consultants to assess its operations and recommend changes. Shortly thereafter, in November, Andrew was pulled from his cashier station and was told to start stocking shelves. His manager explained that the store needed more stockers through the busy holiday season and that he would return to his cashier position in January. January came and went, as did February. As Andrew was signing into work one day, he spotted a note that instructed his manager not to put him on cash. It became apparent to us that the company was discriminating against him, not wanting a developmentally disabled employee with a speech impediment interacting with customers on the front line. He ran home crushed, crying that it wasn't fair. And he was right. Irate, I wrote a scathing letter to the company's head office. He was immediately placed back on cash.

While he was pleased to be back as a cashier, Andrew's trust had been broken and he was never as happy as he had been. He had several panic attacks at work in which his heart started pounding very fast, he felt faint, his body trembled and shook, and the colour drained from his face. I explained to his manager that he was stressed and that she just needed to call me to come and calm him down. Unfortunately, she had no interest in developing a partnership with us.

These early employment experiences led me to reflect on what the world of work would be like if more employers enthusiastically hired developmentally disabled individuals and provided the needed accommodations and training. There is no question in my mind that if they adopted and embraced a strengths-based perspective, they would benefit from an employee like Andrew who is extremely hard working, loyal, reliable, and dependable, with an upbeat, positive attitude, and who is always happy to go to work. And, as we have observed at Andrew's places of employment, the benefits expand beyond those just to the employer and to Andrew, as he infects his co-workers across the workplace with his enthusiasm and commitment to doing a great job.

MEETING MRS. ROBINSON

───

While Andrew continued to struggle with his challenges, he also experienced some home runs.

Since he was a boy, Andrew had loved the Toronto Blue Jays baseball team. He and David regularly attended baseball games together at the SkyDome. Their tradition was to arrive ninety minutes before each game to watch batting practice. Andrew got to know most of the players, umpires, photographers, and staff.

The Blue Jays organization bent over backwards for their special-needs fans. Andrew was once invited for a tour of the locker rooms and the dugout and allowed onto the field during batting practice. He built a special relationship with the director of player safety, and he had the opportunity to meet the president and chief executive officer of the organization. He had a particular adoration for Carlos Delgado, who played first base for the Jays between 1993 and 2004, and had his picture taken with him at the SkyDome when he was nine years old.

Beyond the Jays, Andrew viewed Jackie Robinson as his hero. He had always seen parallels between Jackie, who had broken the colour barrier in baseball, and himself, breaking barriers for disabled people. He read everything that he could about Jackie and watched old videos of him playing ball.

He and David visited the Baseball Hall of Fame in Cooperstown, New York, on several occasions. Both of them looked forward to these visits and came home filled with stories and pictures of the plaques of many great baseball players, including Jackie Robinson. They also got to watch some games at the famous Doubleday Field stadium. But the biggest benefit to Andrew was the time that he got to spend with his dad.

The Jays have been Andrew's get-away for as long as he can remember, and he is emphatic that the team saved his life during his darkest days by providing him with such happiness. "When I was going through my worst mental health challenges, going to a Jays game I could escape reality for nine innings, for three hours, and be myself," he recently wrote me. "There was no judgment, there was no OCD, there was no autism. There was just me being a kid. There was just me living my life."

Andrew didn't just love watching baseball, he loved playing it as well. He played for our local recreational league for years. I remember one nail-biter in which the coach, a kind father of one of the players, sent Andrew in to pitch the last inning of a close game. While I was nervous, Andrew was confident and struck three players out in a row, winning the game for the team. He was hailed as the team's hero that day.

As Andrew's twenty-first birthday approached, I wrote to Rachel Robinson, Jackie Robinson's widow, to ask if she would meet him for his birthday. I described Andrew in my request, and she responded that while she didn't see visitors anymore due to her advanced age, she would make an exception for Andrew.

The next time Andrew visited my mother in New York, they went to see Mrs. Robinson. He was beyond excited and rushed into her apartment to meet her. They talked for over an hour, and she sent him home with a signed book, pictures, and other memorabilia. He couldn't stop talking about the visit for months. And to this day the items that Mrs. Robinson gave him proudly sit in places of honour in his condo for all visitors to see.

A PLACE OF HIS OWN

As Andrew neared his twenty-second birthday, we started looking into supportive housing for him. We were shocked to learn from other parents and organizations involved in housing for the disabled that the wait list for government-funded housing for developmentally disabled individuals is often well over ten years. We were in no hurry to move Andrew out of our house, even though his constant chatter and need for reassurance were exhausting, but we thought that it would be in his best interests to get his name on these wait lists to secure his future. We knew that he lacked the capability to care for himself and that he would need support.

By this time, Andrew's diagnoses were best characterized as pervasive developmental delay (now reclassified as autism spectrum disorder by the American Psychiatric Association's *Diagnostic and Statistical Manual of Mental Disorders*), with significant anxiety and impulsivity, along with Tourette syndrome and ADD. His changing diagnoses did not greatly affect David, me, or Andrew; we had long suspected he was autistic, and the relabelling did not surprise us. For some parents, however, a diagnostic change can be jarring and make a significant difference, as it affects not only decisions concerning medications and therapy but how best to support the child at home and at school. Diagnoses are often moving targets that change over time, particularly as children grow and can often express themselves to a greater degree. But I also learned that if a diagnosis doesn't feel right to trust my gut and keep looking for validation of the issues and behaviours that I observed. We parents live with our children and know them best.

Our search for supportive housing wasn't very fruitful at first. As he had done in the past, Andrew "fell between the cracks." He didn't fit into homes catering to individuals with severe, non-verbal autism, and other settings didn't provide enough support. He couldn't live independently yet equally didn't need full-time supervision.

Through continued research and interaction with mental health professionals and parents, I found a relatively new private group home about ten minutes' drive from our house. The family that owned the building had a daughter with mental health challenges and had retrofitted it into a lovely setting, with sun-filled one-bedroom apartments, a spacious ground-floor kitchen for group meals, a large recreation room, and a backyard patio for barbecuing. At the time, there were just three other residents. The environment was supportive, with full-time and overnight staff willing to work in partnership with us. There was also a nascent activity program, with music, art, and cooking classes. The only downside was the cost, which was in the tens of thousands of dollars per year. David and I both felt strongly that it was worth sacrificing vacations and other luxuries to provide for Andrew's future.

About one year after we had started our search, Andrew moved into a bright one-bedroom apartment on the second floor of the private group home. As he had at both summer camp and at Eagle Hill, he didn't bat an eye leaving home and the transition was seamless. The staff were understanding and fun, and he became particularly close to both the program director and the building superintendent, who provided some male joking and levity. I surprised him with cheery furnishings from IKEA that made him feel like an adult. He loved watching fire trucks, police cars, and ambulances zip by on the busy street below. We spoke with him multiple times a day and saw him several times a week. From the first day, he informed us that he wanted to stay there for life.

As he moved to his new home, Andrew also secured a transfer to a franchise store owned by the grocery chain he worked for. This store was right across the street from his new apartment and was smaller, with more caring staff than the store near us. The owner worked in partnership with us, was able to give him individualized attention, and accommodated his needs by ensuring there were no night shifts on Andrew's schedule. It didn't take long for customers to start flocking to Andrew's line again.

I vividly remember when the owner told me that he received more emails and calls complimenting Andrew than all his other employees combined. When I told Andrew, he was obviously pleased but informed me that his goal was not to receive the most compliments but to make a difference in someone's day.

HEALTH CHALLENGES

—

That year, at age fifty-six, I was diagnosed with breast cancer. This was a surprise: I had had a lump near the front of my left breast for years, but it was regularly tested and was benign. I also went for annual mammograms, which had never detected anything abnormal. After the lump started to grow, however, my doctors identified a malignant tumour hiding behind the lump. I took the diagnosis in stride: I don't know why I was never scared or overwhelmed, but I approached cancer as I do most things in life, with pragmatism and realism, and was confident that treatment would be successful.

Over the next year, I successfully underwent four operations, including a double mastectomy, chemotherapy, and radiation. I had to take a one-year leave from my job but spoke with my executive assistant every day and tried to continue with my life as much as usual while dealing with the constant and stressful care that the children required.

With my oncologist's blessing, I did not isolate myself from others and regularly took the subway, worked out in the gym, and played competitive bridge. With my bald head, I was almost always offered a seat on the subway. I found that much of a patient's progress was mental; my outlook was consistently positive due to my confidence. I only became upset when the IV nurses couldn't find any more workable veins in my arms and caused me pain (they finally inserted a port in my upper arm to solve that problem).

It was interesting to see how differently the children reacted to my diagnosis. Andrew was supportive throughout my year of treatment while not fully understanding the gravity of the situation. He was initially worried but as soon as I reassured him that I wasn't going to die and would be able to continue taking care of him, he relaxed. He eagerly participated in the hospital's annual cancer walk that summer with about twenty other family members, friends, and work colleagues, ingeniously coming up with the team name Stew Crew. Good or bad, he was largely oblivious, and my cancer didn't affect him significantly. Ainsley was much more aware of the risks and was scared. She was going through a particularly rough time of her own, but she tried to put on a brave face and stayed close to me.

There was, however, a bit of levity. After one of my surgeries, I developed lymphedema, a condition in which my left arm and hand swelled due to my compromised lymphatic system. I underwent specialized treatment and started to wear compression gloves and sleeves to control the swelling. Andrew and Ainsley delighted in calling me "sausage arm" during the day and "giraffe arm" at night due to the pattern that the night garment temporarily left on my arm.

Upon completing treatment, I made the decision not to undergo reconstructive surgery. My breasts had never been a major part of my identity. And when I went to the bra store to purchase prosthetic implants to insert in my bras, I found it hysterical that the smallest prostheses were actually larger than my breasts had been pre-cancer!

I knew that my cancer was a serious illness, but I equally knew that my children faced deeper, lifelong adversity. That knowledge kept me grounded throughout my journey. I had to be careful not to be cavalier when speaking with other patients so as not to minimize their experiences. Every person reacts and responds to cancer differently, and it was important to me to let everyone be heard. Given my attitude, the hospital asked me to meet with several patients and their families to encourage them and cheer them on. I was happy to contribute.

GUARDIANSHIP

While I was undergoing chemotherapy, David and I started the complex process of becoming Andrew's legal guardian. Although Andrew was legally an adult, he lacked the capability to make responsible personal or financial decisions, including handling money. The fact that he was friendly with strangers, was overly trusting of everyone, and looked vulnerable with his mouth hanging open, saliva drooling, and eyes shaded made him an easy target. We wanted to keep him secure and protect him from any negative influences.

Guardianship protects those who lack the capability to take care of themselves. It is a legal process in which the guardian becomes the individual's authorized decision maker. There are two major types of guardianship for adults in Ontario: guardians of property, who manage all of an individual's property, including real estate, bank and investment accounts, and other financial accounts and decisions; and guardians of the person, who make decisions regarding health care, nutrition, housing, clothing, hygiene, and safety. We opted to apply for both, as Andrew needed substantial support in all aspects of his life.

David and I carefully explained guardianship to Andrew. It was important for us to ensure that he was comfortable with having guardians. We reviewed all the necessary documents with him and reassured him that he would be better protected and secure. If we were not sure that he understood some wording in the paperwork, we reviewed it again with him. He was fully supportive.

The process was fairly onerous. Working with a trust and estate lawyer, we had to file a petition with the Superior Court of Justice. The petition included a description of Andrew and his disabilities, his level of functioning, and his lack of decision-making capabilities. We had to include affidavits from Drs. Biederman and Davy that attested that Andrew lacked the mental capacity to care for himself. And we had to draft a financial management plan, as well as a guardianship plan for the management of his health care, nutrition, housing, clothing, hygiene, and safety. Our lawyer attended a hearing before the court on our behalf, and, as required, a representative of the sheriff's office came to our house and authoritatively told Andrew, "You have been served." This was jarring to all of us as none of us had ever been served any legal papers before. We had prepared Andrew for this event, and he was actually delighted that an officer of the law had come to speak to him. But it also showed him the seriousness of the guardianship in ensuring his future safety.

Nine months after we started the process, David and I were appointed Andrew's legal guardians. Guardianship is a major responsibility, and one that we believe is well worth it. We must send the court a detailed accounting of Andrew's annual disbursements and receipts, which the court reviews and approves. We appreciate the court's duty to ensure that we are responsible fiduciaries and guardians and do not squander his funds or take advantage of him. I am just relieved that David is a professional financial planner who can take the lead on getting the court all the necessary information.

During this period, we also fully supported Andrew's desire to have a vasectomy. He had been asking for the procedure since he was about sixteen. He was fearful that a future girlfriend might get pregnant, and he didn't want a child to experience the challenges that he had. He also knew that he could not take care of another human being. We agreed, with no conflicting emotions. When he first brought it up as a teenager, his doctors had told him to wait until he was more mature. He continued to ask and when he turned twenty-three, they agreed to proceed. I took him to the clinic, where a number of men were waiting for their procedures. I remember Andrew trying to joke with them about getting snipped or "shooting blanks," which did lighten the mood in the room somewhat. He continued to joke with the doctor throughout his procedure, and I could hear laughter coming from the operating room. After the procedure was complete, Andrew proudly told everyone at his job that he had had a vasectomy. David was a bit embarrassed, but I was amused.

DOWNWARD SPIRAL

———

The first year of the guardianship was relatively uneventful. But then, for no apparent reason, Andrew got it into his head that David and I were trying to stifle his rights. No matter how often we reviewed the paperwork with him and tried to explain, he became upset and angry. He thought he was losing the freedom to live the way he wanted.

That fall, we faced another major challenge. Andrew always wanted the latest electronics and technology and asked us to purchase some expensive software for his computer. He had up-to-date software, however, so we turned him down. His impulsivity overrode reason, and he "borrowed" the credit card of an adult associated with the residence and ordered it. He was quickly found out and we paid restitution, but we were horrified. We spoke at length with Andrew and Dr. Sherman about his behaviour, and he gradually moved from denying any wrongdoing to understanding what he had done. I came to realize that he functioned like a child whenever he got into trouble, initially lying in the hopes of not getting into trouble before admitting what he had done. With Andrew's support, we reinstituted behavioural contracts he agreed to sign that helped him start to slowly recover and settle down. These contracts outlined expectations for him — for example, not going into any store that sold electronic or telecom devices due to his impulsivity, agreeing not to lie or omit the truth when asked a question, and agreeing to work out at least three times each week. He earned rewards towards the purchase of a Microsoft or Apple gift card or points towards a visit with my mother; if he violated any of the conditions in the contract, consequences included losing his spending money saved to date per violation.

A little over a year later, when he was twenty-five years old, Andrew's disorders reared their ugly heads again and he had a horrific year. There seemed to be no obvious trigger for his downward spiral but by June, he was demonstrating unfettered impulsivity and lack of self-control and self-regulation. His overpowering urges led to angry, self-righteous tirades and aggrandizement. He lied compulsively and covered up one lie with another, building a web of deceit that made no sense. For example, he told us that a company was sending him a free phone for having given them valuable feedback. He made repeated calls to different companies to try to get a new computer. Although we had stopped his access to money at the bank and were instead giving him a weekly allowance, he was able to convince the bank to give him some cash. He sent us, particularly me, long angry emails about his rights and how we were violating them, repeatedly threatening to call the police. He constantly name-dropped, using the names of senior executives he did not know to try to impress others and appear special. He supposedly hooked up online with an older woman and invited her to his apartment. Fortunately, we were able to stop it, but to this day, we do not know if she existed.

It was difficult for me to function during this time. I often felt like I was slowly drowning. I was past being worried, frustrated, or resentful. It was too much to handle, and I felt numb. I found myself returning to autopilot mode just to get through each day.

Andrew hit bottom that summer. We had imposed a consequence in which he lost his Internet connection for three months due to his behaviour. Driven by impulsivity, he went to another resident's apartment and borrowed his WiFi password without his knowledge. His deceit was quickly caught. The resident and his family were extremely understanding, but I was devastated.

Dr. Biederman instituted significant medication changes and recommended that Dr. Sherman introduce a consequence system with shorter-term limits that could be repeated as needed. The goal was to make a point and not be in constant conflict, which put Andrew's back up and escalated his behaviour. Dr. Biederman reminded us to look at Andrew's actions from a child's point of view and not to have any adult expectations of him. He reassured us that Andrew was a moral person whose actions were driven by his impulsivity and lack of self-control and regulation. OCD also played a part: repetitive anxious thoughts fuelled his thinking and actions. His urges were so overpowering that they led not only to these behaviours but to self-righteousness and grandiosity.

Dr. Sherman followed Dr. Biederman's advice and introduced the shorter-term consequence system. Andrew's biggest rewards had nothing to do with the Internet but were tied to seeing my mother in New York City. Similarly, the most meaningful consequences to him were not being able to call my mother or losing his privacy.

Ainsley continued to be Andrew's saviour and role model. She could calm him down when no one else could. We didn't want to place a burden on her but she naturally reached out and surrounded him with her love. She was also firm with him, acting as a seasoned caregiver at times. He listened to her and tried to please her above everyone else. I was extremely proud of her and was encouraged that she would be able to take care of him in the future.

Throughout the rest of that year and into 2013, Andrew gradually regained control, albeit not without issues. He had difficulty differentiating between friends and acquaintances, and believed that everyone was his friend. This became a problem in a relationship with a young man who lived in the next building. Andrew's perception of the friendship was unrealistic, and he over-communicated with the young man to the point that he would reach out to him eight times a day and even showed up at his apartment several times a day. The friend cut off contact and threatened to have Andrew charged with harassment. Andrew just could not understand boundaries. When he was rational, he agreed that his behaviour was out of control and that he needed help. At other times, however, he ranted that he had done nothing wrong, was being controlled, manipulated, and taken advantage of and threatened to report me to the police. Although he never acted on his threats, they continued to wear me down emotionally.

Over the next few months, Andrew slowly stabilized. He increasingly looked back at his behaviour with dismay and sorrow. He kept apologizing to David, Ainsley, and me. My heart went out to him that July when he asked for no birthday gifts except to earn our trust back.

EMPLOYMENT CHALLENGES

———

Back in 2011 for Andrew's twenty-fourth birthday, I had arranged for Andrew to meet then Toronto Police Chief Bill Blair. Andrew had always been enamoured of the police, fire, and ambulance services in Toronto. I didn't know Chief Blair, but I wrote to him, describing Andrew, and asked if he would be kind enough to spend a few minutes with him. To my surprise, Chief Blair's office contacted me shortly thereafter to arrange the meeting. Andrew couldn't believe his luck. An officer picked him up at his residence in a police car and drove him to the chief's office, where David met them. The chief was unbelievably kind. He spent over thirty minutes with Andrew, gave him police T-shirts and memorabilia, and set up a tour of Emergency Task Force headquarters.

The following year, Andrew shared his concern with us that his cashier job had no future upside. He had kept in touch with Chief Blair and asked him for a job; Chief Blair kindly told him that he would look into it. Having no filters when reaching out to others, Andrew then emailed Rogers Communications Inc.'s new chief executive officer, whom he didn't know, and asked to be pointed in the right direction to secure a job with the company. Surprisingly, the CEO responded and set him up with a recruiter at the company. No job materialized, but they agreed to keep in touch.

In early 2015, when Andrew was twenty-seven years old, a social media officer in the Toronto Police Service's Corporate Communications Department contacted me and told me that Andrew had been sending hundreds of social media and Facebook friend requests to officers and Police Service staff. This had raised red flags at the Service. I was scared for Andrew but, fortunately, the officer was understanding. He spent significant time with Andrew and explained the gravity of the situation to him. Together with Dr. Sherman and us, he developed a social media code of conduct for Andrew. He explained the difference between friends and acquaintances, and developed black and white solutions that Andrew could understand. Andrew was not allowed to make any new friend requests to officers. He removed hundreds of police and Emergency Task Force contacts from his social media accounts and was told that he could communicate with only three officers to start. Andrew was so relieved that he was not in trouble with the police that he easily complied.

Although the situation with the Police Service was fairly easily resolved, I still found myself becoming despondent. I wondered if Andrew's misconduct would ever stop. I felt almost resigned to his inevitable cycle of ups and downs and his seeming inability to stop getting into trouble. "Here we go again," I'd say to myself. David often felt the same way, but we propped each other up and reminded each other that he would climb out of whatever abyss he was in.

JOB CHANGE

—

Shortly after the incident with the police, Andrew caught his size 14 shoe on the lip of a cabinet while drying dishes in the residence's kitchen and fell. He was in significant pain and couldn't get up. The staff eventually got him to his bed, but he called us at 1 a.m. and asked for help. We quickly drove down to his residence and felt that he needed medical attention to determine what was wrong. We called an ambulance, which took him to our nearby hospital, and X-rays confirmed that he had broken his left hip. He went into surgery the following evening.

After one week in hospital, Andrew was transferred to a rehabilitation facility for seven weeks, followed by intensive outpatient physiotherapy at the rehab facility. He was by far the youngest patient on the orthopaedic floor, so the staff kindly made the decision to give him a private room. Tests confirmed that his bones were brittle, leading him to additionally be diagnosed with osteopenia. His doctor prescribed the medication Actonel to slow down future bone loss.

The hour it took David and me to drive to the hospital and back each day was oddly a period of respite for us. Andrew had no access to social media or a computer and couldn't get into trouble. I feared that he might become bored, but he was treated like a king by the nurses and staff, and he was content.

And after Andrew had been at the facility for two weeks, he got a surprise visitor: Chief Blair showed up to visit along with two of his deputies. Andrew and he had kept in touch, and he had heard about the injury from a nurse he knew. Chief Blair also shared some good news: he had found a job for Andrew with the Toronto Police that he could start once he recovered. This buoyed Andrew's spirits and helped expedite his rehabilitation.

That fall, Andrew started working for the Toronto Police as a Parking Enforcement clerk. By this time, Chief Blair had left the Service. Andrew was hired with much fanfare as the Service's first autistic civilian employee, and the new chief even personally welcomed him on his first day.

While the Service's intentions were wonderful, they lacked experience with developmentally delayed and autistic employees. I led an education session with the Parking Enforcement team before Andrew started in which I told them about Andrew's strengths and disorders, the importance of being clear with him and of chunking his work into manageable pieces so as not to overwhelm him. They agreed to accommodate his needs by keeping his workday stable from 9 a.m. to 5 p.m., instead of putting him on a shift schedule like the rest of the team.

But they did not know what to do with Andrew, and it was a challenging relationship. He was given very little work to do each day. He became bored with the repetitive clerical tasks that he was assigned and got himself into trouble. Instead of processing tickets one Monday, for example, he threw them into the garbage. He requested access to two internal police programs for which he did not have permission. He sent tweets to the chief.

He constantly greeted and re-greeted fellow employees and either hugged them or engaged in play-punching.

Dr. Biederman explained that people with autism commonly experience frontal lobe problems like executive dysfunction, insufficient screening of thoughts and actions, and the inability to stop/think/reflect. Andrew's child-like lying and grandiosity were aimed at either trying to get out of trouble or seem more important. At home, his anxiety about his job security led to more self-righteous behaviour, demanding his rights and again threatening to file human rights complaints against us. Dr. Biederman, Dr. Sherman, David, and I agreed that the grocery store offered a more realistic job for Andrew, particularly given his strengths in customer service. But Andrew was determined to stay with the Police Service.

In early 2017, the Service finally agreed to give Andrew a trial as a Records Department clerk. While he was busy throughout the day, he was still doing repetitive work that he found mundane. Like all of us, he wanted meaningful work. At the end of the month, he transferred back to Parking Enforcement and was told that the Service would find him a more suitable placement.

After waiting several months for a new role for Andrew, I became increasingly impatient. Andrew's boss admitted to me that he was caught between a rock and a hard place: the reality was that Andrew would have to complete more tedious tasks without any issues for a sustained period in order to earn back enough trust to be able to transfer to a different role. He recognized that these tasks were a recipe for disaster for Andrew.

After another month went by without any change, Andrew became so stressed that he took a short-term medical leave. His increased stress caused increased impulsivity, over-communication, and grandiosity. His OCD reared its head more; he picked his lips until they bled and repeatedly reformatted his computer. He pushed us (unsuccessfully) to buy him the latest and greatest electronics. He sent us long emails, demanding his rights. He went on online dating sites, ignoring Dr. Biederman's, Dr. Sherman's, and our advice that he seek friendships with individuals at his own intellectual level instead of people with university degrees. The cycle repeated itself.

Andrew's lack of social life didn't help his situation. Although he was friendly with the other residents in his building, they were older than he was and didn't share his interests. We looked into various social and recreational activities for him, but it was hard to find a good fit. Andrew either couldn't keep up with classes that interested him, like photography, as he couldn't understand what was being said, or he found the dances and bowling at autism-related clubs too basic for him. This saddened and frustrated me, but Andrew was unfazed as he was happiest staying at the residence, chatting with staff, and speaking on the phone for hours with those close with him.

He also continued to pursue unrealistic women on dating sites. To my amazement, he was never discouraged and kept trying. He did have one promising date with another developmentally delayed woman, but she was too anxious to go on a second date.

Still, there were bright spots during this challenging period. In 2016, Andrew became involved in the national Cops for Cancer campaign. He felt connected to the cause because of my experience with cancer and wanted to raise money that could make a difference for people. His inability to filter served him well in fundraising: he called hundreds of people, from family and friends to senior executives and chief executive officers across the country, to make his fundraising pitch. In his first year, he raised just over $3,000. He remained involved for two more years, and in his last year of fundraising, he raised over $20,000, far ahead of the second-place winner.

POSITIVE LIFE CHANGES

———

In 2018, after almost ten years at his residence, Andrew asked to find a new place to live. The people who were moving into his residence needed less support, and the residence was becoming a more transitory environment. There was an emphasis on independence, but what Andrew needed was protection and security. He was less happy there as a result.

David and I supported Andrew's request. I searched for months but could not find an appropriate group setting at his level that had an opening. Instead, we decided to rent him an apartment near us. We found a boutique building five minutes from our house where the owner of a sunny, quiet, one-bedroom unit was looking for a tenant. The owner knew nothing about autism. He interviewed all of us carefully, spoke to references — including two very supportive police officers — and agreed to rent Andrew the unit.

Andrew enthusiastically made the transition.

David and I developed written agreements that we hoped would help ensure Andrew's safety and control his impulsivity. For example, Andrew agreed to obtain our consent before bringing anyone to his place, with the exception of a list of pre-approved visitors, and to get our approval before purchasing any item over $25.

To further support him, we hired a respite worker to provide companionship, cook him dinner every evening, and prepare the next day's meals. Andrew was tired when he got home from work, however, and didn't enjoy engaging with her. So David and I started taking turns going to his apartment every morning to help him prepare for the day. We made his meals, gave him his medications, and ensured that his clothes were clean for work. We checked that he had made his bed, brushed his teeth, and remembered to put on deodorant. We took Saturdays off, and Andrew was happy on his own those days, receiving quick phone reminders from me to take his medications, do his laundry, and eat well.

While on leave from the police that summer, Andrew finally came to the conclusion that he should leave the Service. I cheered his decision and helped him understand that he could continue to be a strong supporter of the police without having to work for them. Two months later, he was hired as a service desk technician at Rogers Communications. He had kept in touch with the recruiter and IT team since meeting with them a few years previously, and they were excited to bring him on.

Andrew's previous employment situations had taught me how to better advocate for him. I clearly communicated the conditions Andrew needed to succeed, and the company was more than willing to accommodate him. Before he started, Andrew and I met with his boss and other team leaders in IT, Human Resources, and Wellbeing, and we talked about his profile, his strengths and his challenges and how they could best support him to be successful in his new role.

I told Rogers that Andrew was a hard worker, kind hearted, and loyal. I added that he seeks to please and has a great sense of humour but that they should be prepared for him to take more of their time than non-disabled employees. I described his disabilities, which largely present through impulsivity and anxiety on the job, and pointed out that he appears to need less support than he does, which can be deceptive. I outlined his difficulties understanding lines of authority, job-appropriate social and behavioural skills, and co-workers' cues. I asked them to chunk his work into smaller pieces, to check and monitor his work regularly, and to be clear and direct with him.

In addition, I emphasized that he needs certainty and closure by the end of the day if something goes wrong or his anxiety will escalate. They laughed when I told them that they should feel free to tell him to stop talking if he chats too much and that he doesn't personalize any of it. And I discussed the fact that he needs reminders about maintaining eye contact and sitting with his head up, as well as about cleaning his mouth if he drools or if his food is messy. I concluded by stating that he is a behaviour modification dream who responds to praise and who wants and needs to know how he is doing regularly.

The team members asked many questions during our discussion. These ranged from what to do if they didn't understand Andrew's speech (my response: don't be afraid to ask him to slow down, repeat what he has said — even multiple times — and/ or lower his voice) to how to tell Andrew not to hug them (my response: simply tell him that you are not comfortable with hugging; he will understand and again not personalize it).

From these discussions, the company hired Ready, Willing and Able, a national employment program that educates and supports employers in hiring and retaining individuals with intellectual disabilities and autism, to act as a job coach, and assist with Andrew's integration and ongoing work. Rogers developed a productive partnership with Ready, Willing and Able and me from the start. And Andrew's boss, Zakir Jaffer, became a role model who has supported him from the day he joined Rogers; he guides Andrew, is firm but fair, and gives him regular feedback, praise, and suggestions on how to improve.

Andrew's goal is to be the best employee at Rogers, not the best disabled employee, and he hopes to stay until he's seventy.

BEHAVIOUR ESCALATION

———

By the spring of 2019, at almost thirty-two years of age, Andrew needed to change therapists. He and Dr. Sherman had outgrown each other after over twenty years together, and the relationship was less productive. This is not an uncommon occurrence between therapists and clients. Andrew had grown and matured. They seemed to go around in circles with one another, with little progression. David and I believed that Andrew needed less intensive therapy, at least for a while. Ready, Willing and Able referred us to an autism consultant who initially provided Andrew with dating advice. Andrew appreciated the consultant's direct approach and asked him to become his life coach. They agreed to meet or speak on the phone monthly.

Although his relationship with the consultant was a good one, Andrew's behaviour at home slowly started to escalate again in late 2019. It reached a peak that November, when he asked for a new computer and said that he would contribute financially. We consented and lent him the money. But the burden of being in debt caused him such heightened anxiety that his body trembled and he started lying about the littlest thing — for example, that he had not used his saved-up allowance to buy airpods (which we then found in his bedroom). Owing money made him distraught.

I should have recognized debt as a stressor and never put Andrew in that position. But I had foolishly relaxed my vigilance, at least temporarily. We immediately took him out of debt by fully paying for the computer, and he agreed not to ask for any other major purchases over the next two years. This seems to have been a watershed moment for him as well, as he finally started to understand and value the benefits and protection offered by his guardianship. He reaffirmed to me how much he appreciated not having to worry about money, get into debt, or make burdensome decisions. He started joking about it, especially when I asked him to do chores like making his bed. "But Mom, you're my guardian," he'd joke.

Soon after this episode, Andrew started complaining that his impulsivity and OCD were escalating. He kept asking to purchase technology that he didn't need and was having difficulty stopping himself from repeatedly reformatting his computer. Dr. Biederman added the tricyclic antidepressant Anafranil to his coterie of medications, which gave Andrew the needed cushion that he needed to function better.

I am often asked by other parents seeking help for their children what medications Andrew takes. I explain that his medications have changed over time and that we have experimented with both increasing and decreasing dosage levels as well as eliminating and replacing medications, some successfully and not. For example, Andrew had taken up to 8 mg of Risperdal twice a day at one point; we tried to gradually decrease this to 4 mg twice a day, but he started to become unstable, with increased mood swings, leading Dr. Biederman to increase it to 6 mg twice a day. Andrew was able, on the other hand, to handle a decrease in his ADD medication Concerta from 54 mg a day to his current level of 18 mg. We recognize the delicate balance and interplay between the medications, and I often find myself holding my breath when his medication cocktail seems to be working well, as it is now. They currently include these:

- Fluvoxamine for OCD: 150 mg twice a day
- Concerta for ADD: 18 mg
- Risperdal for mood: 6 mg twice a day
- Clonazepam for anxiety: 3 mg twice a day
- Anafranil for OCD: 25 mg twice a day
- Actonel for osteopenia: 35 mg DB once a week
- Calcium tablets and a multivitamin pill twice a day

TAKING THE STAGE

As Andrew re-stabilized, he became active as a mental health ambassador. He joined Rogers's Persons with Disabilities committee, participated on a panel for the company's Mental Illness Awareness Week, and was featured in a company-wide video campaign on inclusion. He participated on a team that won a corporate Inclusion and Disability Award, as well as on a team cited for business excellence. He is extremely proud of his advocacy work, as we are. We recently surprised him by securing a framed poster of the video campaign that features him.

In 2019, one of Andrew's superiors invited him to be interviewed at a quarterly speaker series north of Toronto. His superior had co-founded this platform, with the mission of bringing people and communities together through inspirational and enlightening stories. Andrew and I worked together to prepare notes on what he wanted to say about his experiences and the advice he wanted to share with others facing adversity.

Andrew was one of eight speakers invited to speak about their journeys. The audience was packed with people who regularly came to these events, along with a number of Andrew's co-workers and us. When it was his turn to speak, the emcee introduced Andrew as a mental health ambassador, advocate, and trailblazer who has never let his complex disabilities stop him from pursuing his goals.

As I watched Andrew being interviewed on the stage, I was so moved. He told the audience that he has never missed a day of work or of school due to his disabilities and doesn't let them get in his way. Instead, he focuses on his abilities and perseveres. He talked about how the Blue Jays were his escape growing up and allowed him to just be a normal kid. And when he was asked what advice he would give to someone going through their own challenges, he said, "Don't be afraid to reach out for help. Don't feel ashamed. You will feel afraid, don't get me wrong; you will go through some very dark days. But there are also great days that will get you through. Reach out to your family, a friend. Reach out to your psychologist, someone that can help. Someone can listen to you. Someone will be there for you. Don't give up: I guarantee someone will listen." He received a standing ovation.

ANDREW TODAY

When the pandemic hit in March 2020, Andrew and his Rogers' team members started working from home. I was impressed with how well Andrew handled the transition. I feared he might crumble, missing the work environment and the socialization that the office provides. He did become frustrated, complain, and cry from time to time but had no major problems. This period was oddly calm, like his time in the rehab hospital with his broken hip, as he could not go out and be tempted by external influences that often heighten his impulsivity.

In April 2021, David and I bought Andrew a one-bedroom condo in the building in which he was renting. I decorated it with large baseball posters and art that he adores, including three vintage baseball posters from the 1800s. Owning property gives him the long-term security that he needs. The building is right across the street from our local fire station, and Andrew enjoys greeting the firefighters. And he is thrilled that the unit overlooks busy Yonge Street, which gives him a front-row seat to all the action as police, fire trucks, and ambulances race by.

Andrew continues to dislike disruption in his daily life. This is not atypical of individuals with his disabilities, as change and transition are difficult for them and routines are comforting. He dislikes all travel, except for his and David's trips to Florida for the Jays' spring training camp. And as much as he enjoys seeing family in the Laurentians, he prefers to remain in Toronto. This means that at Christmas and during the summer, our family splits up: I stay home with Andrew while David and Ainsley go to David's family cottage in Quebec. I enjoy the cottage but am equally happy staying at our house in Toronto and enjoying some alone time. Because of this, our family celebrates an early Christmas in Toronto, and on Christmas day Andrew and I make a special home-made Christmas brunch and watch movies like *Bad Santa*.

Andrew's favourite hobby is to make videos of our lives together. He stitches together family photographs and weaves in music. They are beautiful videos, which I proudly share with as many people as possible. He also has an unbelievable memory, which can cause me problems because he remembers everything that I say. He often emails family trivia quizzes to David, Ainsley, and me, with questions like "What was the make and model of my first computer?" and "What is Blue Jays' player Carlos Delgado holding in his hand in his picture with me?"

Andrew's inability to filter causes both amusement and consternation. When he was about thirty years old, he went through a phase wondering who was Jewish. He was just curious, as he has no understanding of religion or what it means to be Jewish, Muslim, or Christian. He asked us if our friend Sol Bernstein was Jewish and when we told him that he was, he asked how we knew. No one takes offence, realizing that he is asking with no malicious intentions. And another time, he and I walked into a handbag store where the two female owners greeted us, speaking with accents. He asked them if they were from Argentina ... and they were shocked by his accuracy!

Andrew continues to struggle to understand idiomatic speech. A colleague of mine kindly offered to meet him for dinner one evening right before the pandemic. As Andrew sat on a radiator to wait for him, a passerby jokingly asked him if he had been stood up. Andrew replied, "No, I just sat down."

Andrew's physical health concerns me. His posture remains poor. His head and neck are almost always hanging down, putting his neck and back at risk. With his osteopenia, I worry that he is an accident waiting to happen. He sees a physiotherapist at work as needed, and although he doesn't enjoy physical fitness, he has started working out with a trainer. He also sees a specialty dentist for developmentally disabled patients twice a year, as he is prone to significant tooth decay due to his difficulty effectively brushing his teeth, as well as to his tendency to breathe through his mouth and drool. Additional dental complications come from the effects of his medications on his saliva and on the dryness of his mouth. He has worked with a nutritionist to learn to eat more healthfully: after all those years of drinking milkshakes twice a day when he was too thin as a teenager, he has grown into his body and actually gained thirteen pounds from all the Timbits and treats at work.

Although Andrew has been doing better, we realize that his cycle of good days and bad will continue to repeat itself. Andrew himself recognizes this. He recently acknowledged that he needs more enhanced support from a professional psychologist trained in anxiety and impulsivity, rather than just in autism, to help him with his day-to-day life challenges. Through Tourette Canada, we were introduced to MindFit Health, a psychology clinic with a number of professionals trained in Andrew's various disorders. Dr. Sandor has also told us that he is nearing retirement and kindly referred Andrew to a highly regarded Canadian psychiatrist with expertise in Tourette syndrome and developmental disorders.

Andrew has voiced concern about who will help Ainsley take care of him after David and I die. He has great confidence in her but worries that she may become overwhelmed. We are concerned about this as well. We reassure him that he will be well looked after, not only financially but emotionally and in every other way. David and I have created detailed guardianship documents that outline how Andrew's care should be handled when we are gone. Ainsley will oversee his personal care, with the advice of Andrew's boss, Zak. A family friend who is an investment executive will handle Andrew's finances.

As Andrew ages, the emotional and intellectual gaps between him and his peers widen. His peers continue to mature and take on increasing responsibilities for spouses, children, parents, and houses while Andrew remains frozen in time, like a child in many ways. He looks forward to me waking him in the morning by singing "Five Little Ducks" and similar children's songs. One of his current favourites is a song I made up called "Silly Goose":

> You're a silly goose
> You smell like a goose
> Sometimes you jump
> Sometimes you run
> But you always smile under the sun

It makes him happy and sets him up to have a great start to his day..

Andrew believes that every person he meets is his friend. I call him Mr. Mayor: wherever we go, people know him and call out to him. He recently had his hair cut and, as is his custom, he chatted with everyone in the barbershop. When he got up to pay, the barber told him that another customer had just paid for him. He always strikes up conversations with people on elevators or in the subway. After they get over their initial surprise, they are unfailingly charmed by him and engage with him, even though his speech impediment makes him difficult to understand. A few months ago when he and I were on the subway, a well-dressed man approached me after I got off the train and extended his hand with a $50 bill. He explained that he was in awe of the interaction between Andrew and me and wanted me to use the money to buy something for my son. I was amused and thanked him but explained I couldn't accept the money. Andrew tends to have that effect on people.

Dr. Biederman recently told Andrew how pleased he is with his progress and how glad he is that Andrew can prosper and have access to a full life with the right supports. This charming young man who embraces life is at his best when he feels safe and protected. He knows that those around him love him, and he gives us all much love in return.

part two

AINSLEY

THE EARLY YEARS

Ainsley was born in 1989, twenty-two months after Andrew. She was an adorable, happy baby who seemed to gurgle and smile almost all the time. She ate and slept well and was a far easier baby than her brother.

Ainsley reached all her developmental milestones within the normal time periods. David and I were not too concerned that she might exhibit Andrew's challenges. Andrew was still young at the time, and the advice we were getting from our pediatrician was that there was nothing wrong with him.

As she grew into a toddler, Ainsley's mischievous streak began to show, and it became clear that she was a risk taker. When she was three years old, she decided that it would be fun to be Peter Pan. She "flew" off the top of our main staircase, shouting with joy as she landed with a bang at the bottom of the stairs on the foyer floor. She was extremely lucky to only sprain her ankle, and she smiled impishly and was quite proud of herself in spite of the injury. The incident earned her the lifelong family nickname "Bird."

People were attracted to Ainsley's energetic and bubbly nature. Strangers stopped and admired her rosy complexion, gorgeous reddish-blond hair, and big blue eyes. When the children flew with me to Montreal to see their grandmother when they were two and four years old, I had one of those nightmare flights: unbeknownst to us, Andrew had developed an ear infection and screamed through most of the flight, while Ainsley threw up multiple times, all over herself and me. After we landed, a kind passenger offered to pick up my "adorable daughter" — not so adorable to me with her clothes and hair covered in vomit — and carried her to the terminal while I took Andrew.

Ainsley was also fun and funny. On another flight to New York to visit my mother, she looked out the window and shouted, "So where are the angels?" The passengers around us burst into laughter and applause. Weeks later, she questioned where babies came from, and after her nanny explained that they came from seeds, she asked, "What store sells the seeds?"

As she grew, Ainsley continued to seek adrenaline-generating activities. She loved climbing on climbing frames and furniture, even though we asked her not to. When she got caught, she would be given a time-out and would sit in the corner, weeping and complaining bitterly about the unfairness of her consequence.

Andrew and Ainsley played together well from an early age. They pulled out dresser drawers, emptied them of all clothes, climbed in, and pretended to be Santa and Mrs. Claus on his sled. They sang songs and danced and chased each other around the yard. They also fought like normal siblings, and Ainsley always blamed her brother whenever she misbehaved. But she adored Andrew and followed him around. We didn't realize at the time how much they hopped from one activity to the next in nonstop motion; neither engaged in activities requiring sustained attention, whether colouring a picture or playing with stuffed animals. It all seemed normal to us as theirs was the only childhood behaviours we had experienced since they could walk. The one exception for

Ainsley were the children's book series The Berenstein Bears and Madeleine, which she spent hours devouring.

Ainsley was an early leader among her pre-school friends. They would follow her instructions, whether playing school (she was always the teacher) or hide-and-seek. She became close friends with six girls on our block, and they spent hours at each other's homes. The only area in which she was slow to develop was night-time potty training. She showed no interest in getting rid of her night diaper and resisted our efforts to train her. The first time she was invited to one of her friend's homes for a sleep-over, however, I explained that she couldn't go until she didn't wear a diaper at night. The next night, she was dry and never wore a diaper again.

David and I were delighted with Ainsley. We had a captivating little girl who we thought faced none of Andrew's challenges.

EARLY CRACKS

Ainsley couldn't wait to follow in her brother's footsteps and start school. Once she reached the classroom at our local public school, however, cracks began to show. She couldn't sit still and was disruptive. Her junior and senior kindergarten teachers reported that she could be silly and that her enthusiasm often interfered with her listening and participation. She needed reminders to finish her work and was easily distracted.

In Grade 1, her behaviour in the classroom became less appropriate. She was inattentive, overly chatty, and careless in her work. She shouted out answers to questions instead of waiting her turn. She had trouble staying in her seat and was timed out and sent to the principal's office for disturbing the class almost every day. It was clear that she was having trouble maintaining attention in a large group setting. Even though she was keeping up with her peers academically, I knew that her difficulties were negatively affecting her self-esteem. David and I spent time talking with her and listening, and she told us that she was frightened of losing control. And I was frightened of having another child with special needs. The looming burden seemed overwhelming to face.

We put Ainsley in ballet lessons with her friends, but the rigidity and discipline clashed with her personality and she couldn't or wouldn't follow directions. Instead, she clowned around and made silly faces. We pulled her out after the December holiday concert; we also pulled her out of Brownies, where she was bored. I quickly learned to respect her wishes and put her in activities that appealed to her rather than to me. At her request, she joined an ice hockey team, where she excelled as a goalie for years. A natural athlete, she also learned to swim easily and became a star on her soccer team. David helped coach a number of her baseball, hockey, and soccer teams, and she was so proud to have him there.

Shortly before she turned seven, Ainsley began developing physical and vocal tics, ranging from excessive eye blinking to tongue clicking, and heightened anxiety. We didn't know if she was imitating Andrew or if she was facing these issues herself. She started seeing Dr. Biederman, who diagnosed her with Tourette syndrome, generalized anxiety disorder, short-cycle bipolar disorder, ADD, and learning disabilities. He prescribed the anti-depressant SSRI medication Zoloft for anxiety and Ritalin for ADD. She also started seeing Dr. Davy, as well as a child psychologist who specialized in anxiety disorders at SickKids Hospital.

By that time, I had read and spoken with enough medical professionals to have learned that many of these disorders have a genetic component that runs in families. David and I were therefore not surprised by Ainsley's diagnoses. In fact, I was relieved to learn that, although her issues presented themselves in a significantly different manner than Andrew's, she faced many of the same challenges. This meant that we would more easily be able to understand and provide her with the support she needed. And Ainsley was relieved to learn that her behaviour and lack of control were not her fault and that help was on the way.

We realized how important it was to be transparent with our children and to communicate with them about what was happening at their level. While we fleetingly considered protecting them by not telling them the truth, we quickly rejected that idea: both Andrew and Ainsley were clearly aware of their issues and told us they were scared and wanted help. Being clear, direct, empathetic, and non-judgmental in our conversations helped them understand that they were not bad children, that we were listening to them and validated their feelings. This was critical in establishing the bonds and trust that were necessary to navigate the many challenges to come.

FOUR-LEGGED FRIENDS

As Ainsley turned seven, her emotional and behavioural functioning deteriorated further — at the same time as Andrew's challenges grew. His rages terrified her. She hid in her closet and tried to stay out of his way. She couldn't bring friends to the house because she never knew what behaviours Andrew would exhibit from one day to the next. The chaos at home caused her to feel chaos within herself, and the only way she could get it out of her system was by acting out. She was rude, disobeyed us and her teachers, and could be defiant. She was understandably angry with us for not solving the situation, and she resented the fact that we had to devote so much time to Andrew when he was in crisis, which was often.

We bent over backwards to give her extra attention. We tried to protect her from his rages and outbursts and encouraged her to talk about how she was feeling. We educated her about his disorders and talked about what was happening. Although we did our best, we were exhausted, which meant that we didn't always have the energy to play with her as much as she needed and wanted. Ainsley was overwhelmingly supportive and protective of

Andrew, but his challenges added to her own internal stressors. I feared that she didn't feel as valued or important as Andrew, which broke my heart.

To help, we enrolled Ainsley in a special program at an urban farm in Toronto designed specifically for siblings of families in trauma. It allowed them to have their own time away from their difficulties and provided a safe haven. She loved the support she received, the respite from school and home, and adored helping to care for the animals.

Unfortunately, the program was only temporary. But what lasted was Ainsley's lifelong love of animals. We agreed to buy her a hamster that she named Pickles. I found the rodent unappealing, but she spent hours with Pickles and loved him/her.

When our golden retriever Nugget joined our family, she and Ainsley quickly became inseparable. Ainsley played with Nugget in our back garden, took her for walks and brushed her long coat. Nugget was very patient and allowed Ainsley to dress her up. They even put on plays together. They loved each other, and while we had originally brought Nugget home to support Andrew, the dog played a vital role in helping Ainsley control her outbursts and calm down.

Pets can bring enormous emotional benefits to troubled, vulnerable children. Nugget provided a comforting, soothing presence and unconditional love, lowering Andrew's and Ainsley's stress levels and offering needed companionship. This was true for David and me as well. While caring for Nugget carried a responsibility that was a burden at times, particularly when one of the children was in crisis and needed a lot of our attention, the benefits far outweighed the negatives.

FINDING THE RIGHT SCHOOL

In the winter of Grade 1, Ainsley started seeing a psychologist named Pamela Paris with whom she instantly bonded. We had made the deliberate decision to find Ainsley her own psychologist so that she could feel free to speak openly and be unencumbered by any concern that her psychologist would be biased toward her brother or make judgments based on knowledge of him.

Dr. Paris became one of Ainsley's angels. With her dark wavy hair, lovely smile, and calm, professional demeanour, she instilled confidence in me. And Ainsley responded in kind to her caring, down-to-earth manner and immediately felt understood by her. We knew that Ainsley responded best to those who took an interest in her, while one of her defence mechanisms was to be sullen, morose, and monosyllabic with people she felt didn't understand her. Dr. Paris was non-judgmental and kind, hugged Ainsley on each visit, and listened closely to her. She reflected back what Ainsley said and helped her articulate her feelings so that, together, they could make plans to better control her emotions and behaviours.

This was particularly important because Ainsley faced ongoing criticism from my judgmental mother. My mother was fully supportive of the challenges that both children faced but refused to tolerate unruly behaviour. She informed me that my sister and I had never acted out like Ainsley and that David and I needed to be stricter. Unlike Andrew, who always followed the rules and worshipped my mother's every word, Ainsley could not control her outbursts, no matter how hard she tried. In an ill-guided attempt to turn around the situation, my mother told her on more than one occasion that she was behaving unacceptably and needed to straighten up. Ainsley was wounded and distanced herself. The stark contrast between Ainsley's and Andrew's relationships with my mother further served to exacerbate the situation. Ainsley continued to struggle to gain my mother's approval for years.

Toward the end of Grade 1, we decided to find Ainsley a private school with small class sizes. She underwent a psycho-educational assessment with one of Dr. Paris's colleagues to assist in identifying the optimal school placement. She tried her best during the assessment, but she was restless and inattentive. She kicked the table, chewed her clothes, snapped her fingers, and repeatedly clicked her tongue. She sucked her shoelaces and made rude noises with her arm. She needed frequent breaks. The assessment confirmed that she would benefit from a structured program with small class sizes as her lack of impulse control and her pattern of becoming discouraged and demotivated as tasks became more difficult were causing increasingly problematic and disruptive behaviours.

After some research and conversations with other parents, Montcrest School was at the top of our list. David and I were pleased with its small class sizes, individualized attention, and nurturing. And while academic expectations were high, it was not a high-pressure environment with hours and hours of home-work each day. The principal, Elaine Danson, was caring, open, and transparent. And the school had a special education stream for students with learning disabilities should Ainsley need it later.

Ainsley started Montcrest in Grade 2. She looked adorable in her school uniform comprising a hunter green smock and white shirt, although she hated wearing a skirt instead of pants. She made the transition easily and kept up with the class in all subjects except math. Her teacher observed her cycle of becoming frustrated and then almost giving up, followed by lowering self-confidence. Even simple addition was an overwhelming challenge for her. The teacher also noted that while Ainsley's behaviour could be difficult to control, she was trying her best. Ms. Danson and the teacher's caring bolstered and motivated Ainsley to try to succeed. The school's caretaker also played an instrumental role in helping her calm down many times after she had been sent into the hall for yelling out or some other misbehaviour. He spent time with her, showed her that he cared, and brought a smile to her face, leaving a soft spot for him in her heart.

Finding the right school for any child requires putting yourself in your child's shoes and truly understanding what their needs are. Many parents push their children to attend high-pressure private schools that may or may not be right for them. I have also seen parents resist pulling their children out of these prestigious environments. They want the best for them and mistakenly believe that they will not be accepted into a top university or be able to succeed otherwise.

This challenge is even more difficult for parents with special-needs children. It is critical to understand each child's unique needs and learning profile. Do they need more structure? Would they benefit from smaller classes? More individualized attention? What teaching strategies are used? What student profile does best at the school? What extracurricular activities are offered? And, perhaps most importantly from a parental point of view, how open and transparent is communication with the school? How available are the teachers and principal? How does the school involve parents, therapists, and other caregivers? What strategies does the school use to manage challenging behaviours or bullying? These are the questions that David and I learned to ask as we researched schools for Andrew and Ainsley.

MOUNTING ANXIETY

As Ainsley grew, her anxiety worsened.

The summer after her first year at Montcrest, at age eight, Ainsley and a close friend spent two weeks at an overnight camp in Algonquin Park. Ainsley had been excited to go to camp and spend so much time with her friend. But she became quite anxious as soon as she arrived. She was homesick and cried in her cabin each night. She was so afraid of spiders around the dock that she didn't participate in most swimming activities. The deep darkness at night, thunderstorms, and the fact that there was no counsellor in the cabin with her at all times increased her anxiety. She stayed for the two-week period, but the camp allowed her to call us every day so that we could try to calm her down. We told her we would soon be there to see her and take her home. We realized that her anxiety was increasingly interfering with her life. Once we brought her home, Dr. Davy reminded us that camp was not a requirement for childhood. I was thankful for his healthy perspective.

Later that summer, David and some other fathers took Ainsley and their daughters camping. David was not overly concerned about her anxiety, largely because he would be with her throughout the weekend, and she looked forward to being with her friends. But she freaked out about tiny insects in the tent, cowering in the corner and hysterically crying for David to kill them. When she returned home, she became agitated and nervous whenever she had to go upstairs alone. She became scared that a stranger was in the basement and was going to kill her, and she was convinced she heard someone taking a knife out of one of our kitchen drawers. And she no longer made it through the night at the sleep-overs she had once cherished with friends.

Ainsley's heightened stress took a toll on the entire family. Andrew worried about her, which caused his own anxiety to escalate. Not what we needed! I worked with Dr. Paris to identify strategies to help Ainsley manage her anxiety. We validated her feelings while trying to help her face her fears by articulating the areas in her life that were causing her the most stress. These included a fear of failing her classes and anxiety that family members might become ill and die. She learned deep breathing techniques, and Dr. Paris taught her to visualize her happiest, most favourite places, such as David's family cottage in Quebec, as a way to cope.

Dr. Biederman replaced her Ritalin with another stimulant, Adderall, and introduced Strattera, one of the first non-stimulant medications for ADD. He also replaced her Zoloft with Paxil and prescribed the anti-depressant Remeron and the anti-convulsant Neurontin to further help control her mood and anxiety issues. David and I always ensured that Ainsley understood the changes that were being introduced and the reasons behind them; this had the effect, in turn, of making her feel comfortable enough to give us feedback about how she felt with each change and if the medication regime was working or not.

Over time, these changes brought Ainsley significant relief. The medications provided her with a cushion that gave her brain room to work on her anxiety with Dr. Paris and be open to change.

LEARNING THROUGH CHALLENGES

Even with Ainsley at the right school, challenges remained. At first it was academics. Her anxiety around math continued. She experienced increasing difficulties with problem solving, abstract concepts, and idiomatic expressions like "bite the bullet" and "miss the boat." She couldn't seem to organize her work. Written tests generated fear and tended not to demonstrate her capabilities and understanding of the material. And she engaged in more physical and vocal tics.

The school accommodated her and gave her many oral tests instead, which helped boost her self-esteem. David and I met regularly with her teachers and Ms. Danson, as did Dr. Paris, who provided guidance concerning strategies to help her succeed, whether chunking her work, having her sit near the front of the classroom, or giving her more breaks. The school was pleased to partner with us and repeatedly let Ainsley know that she was a valued student, which made a huge difference in her life and in her view of herself. We knew how critical it was to work as a team to help our daughter and to advocate on her behalf. And although Ainsley's behaviour and academic performance continued to take a toll on David's and my energy, the school's communication and openness importantly gave us increased hope for the future.

Having a good relationship with the school and trust in the education team made it easier to manage Ainsley's growing behavioural challenges. These included calling out, standing on desks, taking other students' lunches if they weren't friendly to her, and swearing.

She also started to experience teasing and bullying. At the start, a few of the students made fun of her and imitated her behaviour. The bullying then escalated to the point that one day, three girls in her class cruelly locked her in a locker. Fortunately, the principal happened to stroll by on a school tour shortly thereafter and heard Ainsley's calls for help. Her good friends defended her, but the bullying was insidious.

Montcrest intervened on her behalf, but Ainsley often cried at night and had trouble believing in herself. Her pain was compounded by the fact that she and her neighbourhood friends had started to grow apart once Ainsley moved schools. She was upset about this, although she tried to hide her feelings. My heart went out to her. Fortunately, Andrew was a great comfort to her and was able to soothe her better than anyone.

One morning, I found the following note on my bed. Ainsley had written it the night before to try to express what she was feeling.

<u>HOW I FEEL</u>
by Ainsley Stewart
March 2000 (age 10)

I feel upset and mad and hopeless I sometimes have a miserable life at times. And at times I am always scared and I am tired of it. The exanity [anxiety] effects...my whole life.
When we got home [yesterday]...I git really scared I thought someone was going to kill me. I also heard a

knife being taken out of its holder. So I kept calling to my Mom I was scared. I do this almost every night and I think it gets my parents annoyed. But anyway I kept calling out I was scared like usal...I think I will always shout out I'am scared and always think some one is going to kill me even thoght my parents have said I will not be scared for the rest of my life Also all my doctors say that too.

The next morning, I had to go sit on the stairs cause I was being bad. When I was about to get some breakfst...I saw this bag that looks like you could sqish it even though I didn't know what it was. Then I saw a knife not a sharp one One that grown ups use to eat with. And I stabbed the bag with the knife and discovered that it was coffee beans. But then I thought really quickly about what I had just done I was in deep deep trouble this time. So Dad grabbed me and put me on the basement stairs again...But then I heard footsteps leading upstairs and discovered that he had walked away on me I guess because I was being rude and bad.

So then I got impacinte so I went to the computer room to type HOW I FEEL. And that's what I am doing right now. Then my Dad came downstairs and we got back toghter again and we turned out fine. So he kissed me and I kissed him goodbye and off he went to work. Then Mom phoned and we turned out to be fine and back toghther too.

Dr. Paris had encouraged Ainsley to express her feelings, whether verbally or in writing, so I was pleased that she had been able to write this note. But it also deepened my sadness for her. I left the office early that day to ensure that I was home before she arrived after school. I told her how proud I was that she had been able to articulate her feelings so well. I wrapped her in my arms and repeated to her over and over again how special she was and that everything was going to be all right.

RETURN TO CAMP

That summer, Ainsley decided to join Andrew at Summit Camp. She believed that Summit would be very different from her previous camp experience because the program catered to youth with challenges like hers and because Andrew would be there for her. To our relief, she had a wonderful eight weeks there. She made friends, won numerous athletic awards — including Athlete of the Summer — and loved having Andrew nearby. Even though she was homesick all summer and wept after we left on Visiting Day, she couldn't wait to return the following two summers.

Summit Camp gave David and me three full summers of relief and distance from the constant wear and tear we faced during the school year. Each summer, it took me a few weeks to adjust to both children being gone, but those eight weeks became critical in refuelling my tank and lessening the burden of the constant vigil that I held. David and I started going out to restaurants and seeing friends, although our greatest joy was most often spent just sitting on our back porch and enjoying the serenity around us.

David and I had the opportunity to think more about Ainsley's growing educational needs while she was away. We had discussed transferring Ainsley into Montcrest's special education class with Ms. Danson numerous times but there were no available spots. We seriously considered moving Ainsley to join her brother at the Douglas Academy, but Ms. Danson thought that Ainsley would do better staying in her regular Grade 6 classes at Montcrest while she awaited placement in special education. We agreed to keep her at Montcrest for the time being. I was a bit frustrated, but I trusted Ms. Danson and knew that she always had Ainsley's best interests in mind.

Ainsley's Grade 6 teacher introduced a number of educational accommodations for her that year. Given her uneven focus, Ainsley often missed or did not understand directions or other important information, so he started asking her after class to repeat back what had been said to ensure she "got" it. He decreased her academic requirements and expectations, including the amount of her homework, and tried to help her learn to slow down and organize her assignments. He understood that her wild behaviour made her scared that she was out of control. A shadow helper was brought in to sit with her during sex education classes so that she would not act out inappropriately. We were pleased with the school's willingness to provide such support, although I was increasingly anxious about the time it was taking to transition Ainsley into special education.

Her teacher played an instrumental role in supporting and nurturing Ainsley and getting her through the year. Nevertheless, she failed all her Grade 6 final exams. Ainsley still remembers how he gently brought her out into the hall to tell her, with tears in his eyes.

In spite of the challenges, there were a number of positives for Ainsley at school that year. Montcrest rewarded her at school assemblies for her athletic prowess on its soccer and softball teams. And she won first place in the school's public speaking contest after she gave an emotional speech about her anxiety: "Some of my fears are that someone in my family is going to die, I am going to die, a kidnapper is going to get me, and my parents are going to have to go to hospital," she said. "These may sound silly, and I know they make no sense, but my brain screams these bad thoughts at me every day."

I was so proud of her ability and willingness to discuss her challenges and increasingly face them head on.

THE LONG-AWAITED TRANSITION

—

Even though Ainsley had failed her exams, Ms. Danson ensured that she passed Grade 6, as she had found a spot for Ainsley in special education the following year. We were delighted, and Ainsley wrote her a letter:

> *To Mrs. Danson, Thank you so much for letting me learn so I couldn't fail grade 6. I really appreciate all the help I got from the teachers and you. I also thank you for wanting me to learn at Montcrest. I also appreciate you for putting me in the special education class next year (I can't wait). But most of all out of the whole year at the end I was having some trouble and you got me through the trouble so I could enjoy school and know I'm cared for and so I could enjoy Montcrest School just like everyone else. At first when my mom told me I was going into the special education class next year I was very upset and didn't want to go to school anymore because I never wanted to leave my friends at school and I didn't want to be different from everyone else. But as my mom and everyone at school especially you explained it more and more to me I relized it wasn't so bad*

and then when everyone helped me through my exams and did oral tests and exams with me ... NOW I WANT TO JOIN RIGHT NOW. So thanks again with everything and I can't wait to be in special education next year.

And what a relief it was. Ainsley loved her Grade 7 teacher, made good friends with two classmates, and became motivated to succeed. Her teacher noted her strong work ethic, positive attitude, and perseverance in the face of multiple challenges. Repetition was key for her, and she needed help generalizing learnings from one area to other areas. She started seeing the school's counsellor and personal coach, who worked closely with Dr. Paris and with us. He showed her that he cared about her, used his sense of humour to help her sort through her behaviours, and was always accessible. She adored him.

The other positive development that occurred that year was that Ainsley acquired some breathing room from Andrew after he went away to Eagle Hill. As close and fiercely protective of him as she was, the fact of Andrew being away gave her a much-needed break and more time to herself. She was particularly pleased when David and I surprised her by taking her to a dude ranch in Arizona for March break. She loved getting up early each morning to feed and groom the horses. She learned to trot and gallop, and David and she took lessons in how to rope horses. She took countless pictures and spent months looking at them again and again. It was one of her happiest memories.

Ainsley's last year at Montcrest was her best year yet. Her Grade 8 teacher affectionately nicknamed her Spider Monkey after a report that she wrote about them. She still became overwhelmed and needed significant support, but she advocated for herself more actively and sought out adults who could help her when she needed it. She worked on strategies to become less disruptive in class, such as proactively removing herself and either going for a walk or sitting in the hall if she felt she was going to erupt or say something inappropriate; these did not always work but she tried hard. She was empathetic and loving with others. The school's counsellor importantly helped her understand that her unique profile meant that not all students would relate easily to her and return her kindness. She continued to be active in most sports.

At her Grade 8 graduation, David and I beamed as she stepped onto the stage. We looked back at her earlier days as a disruptive, out-of-control child who was now starting to gain more control of her emotions and behaviour. We were thrilled at the burgeoning transformation. Ainsley knew that she still faced significant challenges but was proud she was on the right path. At the ceremony, she was awarded the school's Attitude, Improvement and Motivation Award.

GRANDMOTHERS' LOVE

Ainsley gained further happiness as she finally formed a close bond with my mother. As a younger child, she had been stung by my mother's vocal disapproval and critical judgment of her unruly behaviour. I found it surprising and hurtful that my mother couldn't seem to understand the link between Ainsley's behaviour and her disorders. I had tried to speak with her about this on several occasions, having expected her to fully understand, but she had refused to listen to any point of view that wasn't hers.

As Ainsley blossomed, however, they developed a loving relationship. It was Ainsley rather than my mother who changed. She started following the rules to a greater extent and stopped acting out whenever they were together. My mother commented on the transformation in her behaviour and opened her heart to her granddaughter. They talked every day on the phone, laughed, and made plans for Ainsley to visit New York. My mother repeatedly told her how beautiful she was and that she would grow up to be a success in life. She even invited Ainsley and one of her classmates to New York one long weekend, where she was delighted to shop with them and took them to see *Beauty and The Beast* on Broadway.

Ainsley had always enjoyed a warm relationship with David's mother, who was much more of a private woman than my mother. She was less vocal about her concerns for Ainsley and quietly accepted both children. Ainsley implicitly knew that she loved her. As a result, Christmases, March breaks, and summer holidays at her home in the Laurentians were a delight for Ainsley. She loved picking blueberries and playing Go Fish with her grandmother, playing with her cousins when they came, and riding the lawn tractor with Andrew.

I felt it was important for Ainsley to have a close relationship with both her grandmothers. They were not only positive female role models, but provided her with a critical web of support. Although they lived far away, their love and acceptance were instrumental in bolstering Ainsley and giving her the happiness and confidence she needed to embrace her strengths and face her problems head on.

JOINING ANDREW

As high school approached, Ainsley remained well aware of her academic limitations, particularly in math and problem-solving. She suffered from fine motor and graphomotor problems, gripping her pen or pencil (as well as fork or spoon) with a tight fist. She still could not tell time, which embarrassed her. Her medications helped but she was volatile, particularly at home. She would flip from giddy to angry to sad from one minute to the next. We knew that she was sensitive, easily frustrated and highly anxious, which led to her outbursts at home. Dr. Biederman helped us to better understand by explaining that depression is often represented as anger in many children. And while she was able to make friends, she had increasing difficulty keeping them as she missed or misread their social cues or said inappropriate things to them. She slowly lost every friend she had had in the neighbourhood.

Ainsley was eager to join Andrew at Eagle Hill. She had gotten to know the school well over two years of visiting him and believed that it would help her academically, emotionally, and socially. She was attracted to the fact that the entire program was dedicated to students with ADD and learning disabilities, rather than having just one special education classroom as at Montcrest. And she missed being with Andrew. She underwent a psychoeducational assessment to confirm her eligibility. The assessment unsurprisingly concluded that her difficulties with mood and impulse control, as well as with motor regulation, created obstacles to her abilities to sustain attention and absorb information. The assessor recommended placement in small, structured classrooms with program modifications and ongoing social skills training and counselling. Eagle Hill readily accepted her, and she excitedly planned for high school.

Ainsley enjoyed her first year at Eagle Hill, although she reacted to the school environment far differently than her rule-bound brother. She railed against curfews, broke minor school rules such as not staying in her dorm room, and talked back at certain staff members. She continued to have difficulty interpreting what others said, whether in class or socially, as well as misunderstanding their motives and actions when explanations were not available.

Academically, however, she thrived under the school's individualized, multi-modal approach. Her teachers commented on her motivation to do well and her willingness to work hard, particularly in remedial math, which she took two years in a row. The school provided extensive accommodations, ranging from seating Ainsley near the teacher to minimize distractions to providing her with booklists, course outlines, and the schedule of assignments in advance, often with study guides. She was given extra time on assignments and tests, and her teachers prompted her to help her stay focused. They also remained available after class or at other agreed times to give her more individualized help. In addition, she met with the school psychologist weekly and saw Dr. Paris whenever she was home.

Ainsley was also delighted to be able to spend more time with Andrew. They continued to be each other's best friend, and Ainsley increasingly took on the role of the older sibling. Whenever Andrew became stressed, she would be called to come and calm him down. She was often the only person who could comfort him and get him through his anxieties.

BEHAVIOUR TRANSFORMATION

In Grade 10, when Ainsley was fifteen, standardized testing revealed her ongoing significant deficits in math but also showed improvements in word meaning and context. Eagle Hill used these tests as guides and benchmarks that supplemented her teachers' observations.

Ainsley's behaviour continued to be disruptive. She believed that one of her teachers didn't like her, and she reacted by using an inappropriate defence mechanism: she cursed loudly at the teacher when she brought her toddler to class one day, rudely telling her that her daughter was too young to be in the class.

She continued to fight against school rules and the limits placed on her. She snuck out of her dorm room at night by cutting holes in her screen window, slept in friends' rooms when she wasn't supposed to, and acted out during homework time. She swore at the night staff and clashed with her residence counsellor. Her consequences included being "dormed" and "roomed," which meant that she had to stay in her dorm and/or room after dinner all night. She also had to perform community service by joining the Adopt a Grandparent Club, in which she grudgingly visited with seniors at a local long-term care facility. We had numerous meetings and calls with the school. I wondered if she would ever grow up.

One of the most upsetting incidents for Ainsley occurred in her Grade 10 literature class. Some of her classmates knew that she didn't understand the subject matter, and she believed that they purposefully fed her misinformation so they could laugh at her whenever she was called on. After she tried to explain what she had read to the teacher, he told her that she obviously had not done the reading. She retorted that she had indeed done her homework. This pattern continued every week until she grew so frustrated one morning that she disrespectfully swore and shouted at him in front of the class. The teacher sent her into the hall and warned her to never talk to him again that way. She was also permanently kicked out of the class, which, while upsetting in the short term, was a blessing in disguise as she was then placed in a literature class at her level. The teacher — who may likely remember this incident in a different light — and she didn't speak to one another for the next eighteen months. They did, however, reconcile before her graduation.

That summer, Ainsley and David took a trip that further strengthened their bond and also seemed to set the stage for a behaviour change in Ainsley. In July, they travelled to England and Scotland to meet David's relatives and then went to northern France to see the grave of David's grandfather, who had been killed near Vimy Ridge. They shared a strong interest in World War I and in family history, and Ainsley was able to learn a lot on the trip. She loved meeting her relatives and visiting the war graves. The visit to Vimy was particularly meaningful to David, whose last visit to the site had been when he was Ainsley's age. Ainsley's behaviour was stellar throughout the trip, and David told her repeatedly how much he enjoyed being with her. It was a trip and a bonding experience that they both still talk about to this day.

In Grade 11, Ainsley's behaviour did indeed turn a corner for the better! Time and maturity seemed to be the answer for her. Unlike many of her peers who morphed from sweet young girls into rebellious teens, Ainsley softened in the latter half of high school. She continued to dislike authority but came to better understand its importance. She developed improved relationships with the faculty and staff. She complied to a much greater extent with the rules and reached a truce, albeit an uneasy one, with her residence counsellor. Her teachers noted her more positive attitude and the fact that she rarely talked back. She was proud of her ability to advocate for herself in more appropriate ways. She sought assistance and improvement in being patient when her teachers were busy and could not help her right away. She more often recognized when she missed information and realized the benefits of repeating back her understanding of what had been said. And physically, she blossomed from a rough and tumble tomboy into a beautiful young woman who became interested in boys. I laughed, remembering how my mother had repeatedly told Ainsley and me that this transformation would happen.

By the time Ainsley entered Grade 12, she had become a positive role model and mentor to a number of her peers. She was active in many school activities, from the soccer team to Students Against Drunk Driving, and she was pleased to finally earn Semi-Independent Status, with its privilege of fewer restrictions. Her teachers described her as committed and self-motivated, with the desire to succeed.

GRADUATION

In the spring of her Grade 11 year, Ainsley had completed another psychoeducational assessment for university admission purposes. The assessor noted her academic challenges with math and word meaning, impulse control problems, and social skills deficits. To no one's surprise, he recommended finding a university with a small student–teacher ratio and a strong student support program that would provide her with the full suite of academic accommodations.

Ainsley and I visited a number of universities in the fall of her final year at Eagle Hill. She fell in love with Curry College, a private liberal arts university seven miles outside Boston with a student–teacher ratio of 12:1. It had a beautiful rolling campus and an exceptional student support program. Ainsley had become interested in a career as either a veterinarian or psychologist. She chose psychology, having been inspired by how much Dr. Paris had helped her, as well as by her own ability to help her brother. During the summers, she had also worked as a day camp counsellor for pre-school children and found that she had a natural talent for engaging with them, particularly with those experiencing developmental and emotional challenges. She applied to Curry's psychology program and was excited to be granted early admission.

That June, we attended Ainsley's high school graduation ceremony. Ainsley looked beautiful in her white cap and gown. David's sister and her husband came, along with my sister and one of my cousins and his family. Dr. Paris was a surprise guest. Ainsley was so proud and happy. During the ceremony, the headmaster, whom Ainsley, David, and I held in high regard, read a stanza about each graduating student. Ainsley's poem was as follows:

> *It's the end of an era, a decade or more —*
> *With the Stewarts on campus, life's never a bore.*
> *Ainsley, your words may be sharp from time to time,*
> *But at heart, you're a softy (now that doesn't rhyme!)*
> *From Canada to Hardwick to Curry next year.*
> *You'll do us all proud — you're a true Pioneer.*

While he meant well, his line about her words being sharp stung her. She knew she had grown enormously, and his words made her feel undervalued. We understood that the headmaster had meant no harm, but it would have made such a difference to Ainsley if he had made mention of her transition into a caring young woman who faced extraordinary challenges with grace and maturity. Words carry weight.

OFF TO UNIVERSITY

Ainsley entered Curry with high hopes. She attended Curry's two-month summer program for learning-disabled students right after high school graduation in order to become acclimated and to orient her to the school's student support services before the rest of the student body arrived in September. This served to bolster her confidence that she would succeed.

She and her assigned roommate spoke on the phone before classes started so they could get to know each other a bit. And she and I had fun shopping for clothes and posters for her room.

She jumped into the fall head-first with excitement.

Ainsley enjoyed her first-year classes. She was particularly able to relate to the issues discussed in her introductory child psychology class, using her own lived experiences to implicitly understand and empathize with children facing similar challenges. She took full advantage of the school's student support services and was very pleased with her grades.

Although Ainsley initially did well academically, she had a difficult time socially. She didn't get along with her roommate, who wanted to party all the time, and she struggled to make friends.

The one bright spot was a close friendship she formed with a fellow psychology student named Amy. At the start of the year, Ainsley had spoken with her professor about our family, and he had invited me to speak to the class about Ainsley's perseverance in the face of significant adversity. Amy reached out to Ainsley after the class, and they formed a quick friendship. Ainsley often slept over at Amy's off-campus apartment, and they stayed up all night talking about everything from their career aspirations to Amy's dog.

DATING CHALLENGES

Ainsley didn't realize how beautiful she had become as a teen-ager. I knew that boys would be attracted to her blond hair, big blue eyes, and gorgeous figure. I had a number of serious talks with her about sex, self-respect, and not letting anyone take advantage of her. I knew that she was vulnerable and wanted other people to like her, but I hoped she had the inner strength to hold her own.

As Ainsley herself became interested in boys, she experienced the highs and lows of relationships throughout her teenage years. These experiences ranged from succumbing to peer pressure to have sex with one boy before she was emotionally ready, leav-ing her feeling violated; to enjoying wonderful puppy love with a cute, artistic boy who made her feel valued and protected; to unfortunately experiencing physical abuse.

It takes an incredible amount of courage to stand up to an abuser. Ainsley was so emotionally fragile, lonely, and vulnerable that it took her months to find the courage to break it off. She then felt ashamed that she had let the situation continue for as long as it did.

Unlike many teens, Ainsley confided in me about her relationships, albeit usually after they had ended. I was glad that she felt she could come to me without being judged and that she wanted and needed my advice. We talked at length about sex, consent, and power, and she seemed to absorb it and be more confident about how she would handle future relationships. But I remained nervous about her fragility and neediness and kept my antenna up.

UNRAVELLING

—

Ainsley unravelled at Curry after her last break-up. Her friend Amy was planning to get married and move to Virginia the following year, leaving Ainsley with no friends. She craved acceptance and connections with others and started to confuse sex with affection. Her grades dropped as she found her psychology courses increasingly difficult. She feared that she would not be capable of pursuing a career in the field, and the thought of having to get a PhD overwhelmed her. She still had significant difficulty with math and could not tell time. She started cutting her wrists and arms with a knife as a cry for help. She needed to let us know that she was not okay.

I was frantic with worry. Her emotional health was of paramount importance to me. I couldn't fly down to her as I was undergoing chemotherapy for my breast cancer, but I spoke with her on the phone every day and pleaded with her to come home and get help. She rejected David's offer to come to Curry because she wanted him to stay with me during my treatment; he looks back in hindsight and wishes he had just gotten on a plane and scooped her up.

David and I tried to shield Andrew from much of what was happening so as not to heighten his anxiety, but the children spoke every day, as they always had, and he knew that something was terribly wrong.

We were so thankful when Ainsley finally agreed to leave Curry and move back to Toronto for good at the end of her second year.

COMPLICATIONS

———

I was relieved to have Ainsley home, where David and I could keep a close eye on her and provide family support. It was also lovely for me to have her near me as I was undergoing my cancer treatments.

Ainsley's first year back in Toronto was a nightmare for all of us. Although she was relieved to be home, she was scared of her fragile mental health and knew that she needed intensive therapy. She continued to cut her arms and wrists, and even though she was very worried about my health and stayed close to me, she became physically aggressive and violent with me. This had nothing to do with me but with her internal demons. She erupted into irrational, child-like tantrums every few days. She screamed in my face, held my upper arms in a vice grip, and pushed me. I was physically weak from the chemotherapy and lacked the reserves to protect or defend myself. I found myself steeling my body and trying not to show her how afraid I was. Just as I had during Andrew's rages, I told myself over and over again that this was not Ainsley herself but her disorders speaking.

The frequency and intensity of Ainsley's outbursts increased, and her distress became even more palpable. She couldn't control herself. She was miserable and repeatedly told me that she hated herself. She knew her behaviour made no sense, and it was a surreal experience for her. She particularly feared the intense anger building inside her. She started pulling her hair out and grinding her teeth at night. Her bed was full of hair each morning, and her jaws were sore. On top of this, she began to suffer from persistent nausea.

Dr. Biederman changed her medications several times. He introduced the antipsychotic medication Seroquel, as well as Abilify, another antipsychotic used for mood control, but all it did was cause her to gain thirty pounds, which further intensified her self-loathing. He also started her on clonazepam, a tranquilizer of the benzodiazepine class that targets anxiety and mood. The medication changes were not successful, as they had been in the past.

Ainsley decided that she needed to switch to a Canadian-based psychiatrist who could work closely with her. She also believed that she needed a new psychologist. As much as she adored Dr. Paris, she was concerned that Dr. Paris would continue to view her in the same light as she had as a child, rather than the twenty-year-old she had become. She additionally felt that she needed more intensive therapy. She started working with a Toronto-based dialectical behaviour therapy specialist, a therapy that is often used with those with borderline personality disorder. But she did not fall into this category, and the therapy was too rigid for her and did not work.

I had gotten to know two psychiatrists at Canada's largest psychiatric hospital, the Centre for Addiction and Mental Health (CAMH), through my volunteer work on its board of directors. They helped us find Dr. Jinous Hamidi, a clinical psychiatrist there who became another one of Ainsley's angels. With dark shoulder-length curly hair and big brown eyes, Dr. Hamidi was insightful, empathetic, and compassionate. Although a bit scattered, she bolstered Ainsley's confidence by telling her that she could and would succeed.

To this day, Ainsley believes that Dr. Hamidi saved her life. She met with Ainsley, as well as with Ainsley and me together, on a weekly basis. Over the next several years, she significantly changed Ainsley's cocktail of medications, gradually titrating dosages down and removing Abilify and Remeron. Instead, she slowly introduced Lamictal and Cipralex, two anti-depressants for mood and anxiety. She also started her on the antihypertensive clonidine for ADD and anxiety. We held our breaths and waited. We were so hopeful of a better outcome, yet frightened of worsening behaviours and mental health.

I cannot overemphasize how delicate this process is and how Dr. Hamidi made incremental changes gradually over an extended period so as to minimize the risks of harmful withdrawal and other side effects. Medication changes can play havoc with a person's body. Ainsley suffered long-lasting withdrawal effects after stopping Seroquel, characterized by severe itchiness and nausea. She has never been able to stop clonazepam completely, as withdrawal caused her body to twitch uncontrollably and make her have difficulty walking. Although we were scared of the possible repercussions of the medication changes, we had confidence that Dr. Hamidi was trying to implement changes that would help Ainsley for the long term.

After a year of pure hell, it was as if a light switched on and Ainsley's behaviour turned around. She was able to stop the cutting and violence and to start focusing on herself. She was so grateful when the darkness around her started to lift. And David and I held her tightly as relief washed over both of us.

RETURNING TO COLLEGE

—

With ongoing improvement, Ainsley was able to start thinking about her future and her career again. She contacted her former Montcrest principal, Ms. Danson, for advice about educational options. She decided that a career as a child and youth worker would be a better fit for her than as a psychologist: the educational requirements would be less onerous and the job would provide her with the satisfaction she sought. She successfully applied to Seneca College's Child and Youth Worker Advanced Diploma program and started in the fall of 2009, at age twenty.

Things gradually became easier for Ainsley. She did well at Seneca with the help of a fantastic tutor/coach, and she enjoyed her internships at a group home for teenagers in legal trouble and at a children's residential treatment centre. She learned to better regulate her emotions, social behaviour, and work habits. And she learned to tell time!

She still faced difficulties with math, sustained attention particularly in areas not of interest to her, accuracy, and organization, but she worked hard to address these. Her self-confidence remained shaky and she had no friends. She suffered minor setbacks from time to time, with sudden anger bubbling up inside her and continuing anxiety. She learned strategies to physically separate herself from us during these periods of anger and took clonazepam for anxiety on an "as needed," or PRN, basis to give her some cushion.

In 2012, Ainsley graduated with high honours on the Presidential Honour Roll at Seneca. As she stepped onto the platform to accept her diploma, I teared up. I looked over at David, and he too had tears in his eyes. And she was rightfully proud of herself on this momentous occasion. She had come through such an abysmal period. She had persevered. She looked back on what she had been able to achieve in the face of extreme adversity and, perhaps for the first time in her life, understood how special she was.

ENTERING THE WORLD OF WORK

Upon graduation, Ainsley was hired on contract at the children's residential treatment centre where she had interned. The centre followed the interdisciplinary approach that I had always espoused, working in partnership with all of the children's caregivers. They involved their clients' psychiatrists, psychologists, social workers, child and youth workers, nurses, and respite workers, in addition to the families themselves. Ainsley was comfortable with this approach and settled into her role well.

The centre housed about fifteen adolescents with significant behavioural and mental health challenges. She worked with them both individually and in groups. She introduced behaviour modification and incentive programs, and she co-led group sessions with the girls where they discussed issues such as hygiene and dating. One fourteen-year-old had severe anger and behaviour issues, and Ainsley created meaningful rewards for her that gave her one-on-one time with her favourite staff and were effective at curbing her outbursts. A male client with fetal alcohol syndrome disorder regularly put himself at risk, spending his free time smoking and hanging out on dangerous street corners. Ainsley and her co-workers tried to introduce more productive activities for him and his family like going on walks together. She learned a great deal about being a child and youth worker, and became accustomed to different shifts, from days, evenings, and weekends to overnight shifts. She even took an active role helping the children with their homework, including high school math.

Ainsley consistently received positive performance reviews. Several of the staff became her friends, including a seasoned professional who became one of her mentors. She knew she had found her niche. It was heartwarming to see her enjoy and succeed at her job.

But while her professional self-esteem grew, socially she remained vulnerable and fragile. Finding friends outside work continued to be a challenge, and she made several poor choices in the men she dated. One man lied about his employment, education, and prospects; another tried to get her to pay for all their meals and activities, whether bowling or going to movies. I realized this would be a long-term challenge for her, as she — in her own words — felt "damaged" and believed that no normal man would be interested in her.

ATTACKED

Although Ainsley enjoyed her job, the centre had no full-time jobs available. There were no prospects of any openings in the near future so staying long term wasn't an option. After three years, at the age of twenty-six, she left and accepted a position as a child and youth worker in a group home.

There, she worked with eight pre-teen children who had experienced serious trauma, such as child abuse and neglect and abandonment. This was an age group she hadn't worked with before and exposed her to a different population of vulnerable children. She dispensed medication, coordinated shifts, and implemented behaviour modification programs. One nine-year-old was terrified of going to sleep at night, and she helped him overcome his fears by discussing them openly and facing them for the first time. She de-escalated challenging behaviours using empathy and positive communication; she told the children what she wanted them to do rather than pointing out what *not* to do. She set limits and boundaries, which gave them security even as they railed against the rules. She taught basic life skills such as personal hygiene (brushing teeth, washing hands after going to the bathroom, combing hair) and safety (crossing the street, not talking with strangers). And she worked closely with a ten-year-old diagnosed with multiple complex disorders, a role that was extremely difficult as he was oppositional and hated authority.

Ainsley loved her job and decided to further her education, even though she realized she would likely have difficulty with some of the coursework. She enrolled in Ryerson (now Toronto Metropolitan) University's Bachelor of Arts program in Child and Youth Care on a part-time basis so that she could continue to work.

Her life was on a positive track until early 2016, several months after she had started the job. Shortly after Ainsley arrived for her shift, a large, aggressive pre-teen became belligerent when Ainsley asked him to wait to go outside. This infuriated him, and he ran up to Ainsley and started kicking her hard in the face. She fell to the floor as he continued to pound her face and chest. She was able to yell for help, which caused the boy to stop kicking her for a moment. Another staff member rushed in, and the distraction gave Ainsley a chance to stand up. Together, they tried to hold the boy's arms and escort him out of the room. One of his arms got loose, however, and he punched Ainsley first in the eye and then in the ear. At that point, a third staff member arrived and they were able to get him outside.

There was blood all over Ainsley's hoodie and on the couch and floor. She broke down, started weeping, and realized she had been badly hurt. The bleeding wouldn't stop. She called to let us know that she had been punched by a client and was going to get herself checked out but was fine. She refused to tell us which hospital she was going to as she didn't want to unnecessarily worry us. Of course, that had the opposite effect on me but she was adamant that she didn't need our help.

In shock, Ainsley drove herself to hospital, where she was

diagnosed with a concussion. She also suffered a black eye and a heavily bruised chest and face. She got three stitches above one of her eyes. At that point, she finally called us and told us what had really happened. David and I raced to pick her up. Once she saw our faces, she crumbled. And then I crumbled. I couldn't believe what had happened and was horrified at how beaten up she was. I remember wanting to wave a magic wand over her and make her pain disappear.

Over the next several days, she experienced severe migraine headaches, nausea, and vomiting and developed PTSD-type symptoms, including dizziness, nightmares, and heightened anxiety. Bright lights bothered her and made her symptoms worse. She continually replayed the assault in her head and suffered from flashbacks for a long period. To this day, she cannot watch others fight or beat each other up on screen or in real life.

After three months, she still hadn't recovered enough to go back to work. She also couldn't study and lost the full winter and spring/summer terms at Ryerson.

That summer, after being on the wait list for four months, Ainsley got an appointment at a leading head injury clinic in downtown Toronto. The doctors there initially referred her to a migraine specialist who was not successful in lessening her symptoms. This was followed by a referral to a nearby pain and headache clinic, where she began more successful, long-term treatments for migraines and neck pain with global anesthetic injections and medical Botox.

The stress of having to constantly care for Ainsley, on top of dealing with Andrew, who was extremely upset about what had happened, was unbearable for me at times. David and I shared her caretaking and tried to take turns to give each other a break whenever possible. I knew that I had to just put my blinders on, keep my head up, and persevere, hoping she would continue to improve. One medical professional told me in an admiring fashion that I was like a machine. I didn't know if this was really a compliment, but I felt I had no choice, given my love for Ainsley. I wondered if she — as well as I — would ever catch a break. It seemed so unfair.

MOVING FORWARD ... AND OUT

Ainsley was finally ready to return to both work and her studies that fall, eight months after the assault. She promised us that she would work only with young children in the future.

She decided that she wanted to work in the education system and successfully applied to a nearby school board where she was hired as a child and youth worker. Since then, she has had the opportunity to work at three different grade schools. Her experiences have ranged from working with a five-year-old with serious trauma and oppositional disorders to shadowing a nine-year-old with complex mental health disorders and learning disabilities. She is currently working in a Grade 1 classroom for children with autism. A number of the children in the class are exceptionally bright academically but face significant emotional and behavioural problems.

Ainsley has developed into a highly respected child and youth worker. She has used cognitive behavioural approaches to teach the students how to recognize and identify their feelings, make more sense of them, and better control their emotions. She has used innovative communication tools like

Voice4U on iPads that help the children express their feelings and thoughts. She has introduced coping mechanisms such as deep breathing and has taught basic life skills. And she has honed her skills in applied behavioural analysis, a type of therapy commonly used with developmentally delayed children and those on the autism spectrum to improve their social, communication, and learning skills.

Ainsley works in partnership with the children's teachers, relevant staff members, parents, psychiatrists, psychologists, and social workers, as well as with their respite workers, to ensure that everyone is aligned in the children's best interests. She loves her job and has a passion for helping not only these vulnerable children but their families as well. Her job is her calling, and she is clearly gifted in her field.

In the midst of all this, Ainsley and another child and youth worker decided to become apartment-mates. Sophie and she found a lovely two-bedroom unit in a high-rise building about ten minutes away from our home with a gorgeous view of downtown Toronto. We bought her some furniture and helped move her in. At first she was very happy. Sophie and she became best friends. They bought fish and hamsters together, took Sophie's dog out for walks, and went dancing at clubs. They stood on their balcony at night and playfully called out to passersby. Ainsley seemed to be in a much happier state of mind. She kept the apartment clean, shopped for food, and did laundry. And she studied for her Ryerson courses in her free time.

Shortly after moving in, Ainsley met her next boyfriend through a mutual friend and they fell in love. He was kind, outgoing, and caring, although he had some depression. He lived with his highly religious parents and adhered to their values.

Less than a year after moving in with Sophie, Ainsley made the decision to move back home. While she enjoyed their friendship, their lifestyles differed significantly and she wanted to live in a quieter environment.

The next several months also saw Ainsley and her boyfriend break up. They both knew that they had no future together, largely due to family differences. Although initially upset, Ainsley showed great maturity as she came to understand that these differences would only have become increasingly divisive to them. I had always told her that it was far better to be alone than in a relationship that wasn't right for her. She accepted this advice and focused on her work and studies.

Ainsley still wanted to move out, this time on her own. After several months at home, she was able to find a spacious main-floor one-bedroom apartment in an old house. It was a bit run down, but it was a perfect place to start. It was also only three blocks away from us, and we enjoyed being so close and visiting each other regularly.

Ainsley also realized that she needed more professional help. She was disorganized outside work and found herself unable to complete chores like cleaning, shopping for food, or cooking, things she had been able to do when she was living with Sophie. She didn't know why these tasks had become paralyzing to her. She gained weight from eating junk food and not working out, and she didn't feel good about her appearance. And she was lonely. Dr. Hamidi referred her to a psychologist who advised her to spend less time with us and to meet more people. Ainsley agreed with these suggestions in principle, but she found the psychologist unhelpful in giving her concrete strategies to deal with her anxieties and executive function problems. She stopped seeing her after several sessions and tried to manage on her own.

In 2020, at age thirty-one, Ainsley graduated from Ryerson University with her Bachelor of Arts in Child and Youth Care. She did well in her courses, but the requirement to complete a thesis was challenging. She worked with a wonderful tutor Ms. Danson had found, but her professor gave her a failing grade on her initial draft and wrote unnecessary and puzzling negative comments. She was devastated and feared she would be unable to graduate. I was outraged and, with her approval, contacted the department head on her behalf, as she was in too weak an emotional state to advocate for herself. He met with Ainsley, her tutor, David, and me and readily agreed to become her thesis advisor himself. He also modified the requirements of her thesis, which included a comprehensive literature review, an analysis of the literature, and a section on her personal reflections growing up with a sibling with autism.

"Due to the chaos [with Andrew] at home, I felt chaos inside myself as well, and the only way I got it out was by acting out," she wrote in her thesis. "With all my concerns and the negative emotions and experiences that I have faced, my brother is now my best friend and I am very proud of him. Whenever either of us is upset or in trouble, we turn to each other and are best at helping each other. I admire his friendliness to everyone he meets, his strong work ethic, his sense of humour and his ability to somehow bring out the best in others. He sees the good in everyone, and he has taught me to be caring, empathetic and to want to help others."

She beamed with pride when her professor gave her an A+ on her thesis, as well as on her final grade for the course. I was overcome with emotion at his comments:

> *Ainsley, This is a marvelous piece of work... First, thanks for the honesty; second, if, as you say, this has helped you understand and make meaning of your experiences, then I would say that this project has been a major success! And of course I am pleased and inspired by reading about how as adults, you and your brother have developed into a powerhouse of siblinghood, and that your parents,*

notwithstanding what are undoubtedly major struggles and sacrifices, have managed to get through this and now are surely proud of their kids. As a parent myself, I can only extend my respect to yours, to you and to your brother. Exceptionally well done.

AINSLEY TODAY

About six months after Ainsley moved into her apartment, she fulfilled her lifelong dream of owning a dog. After much research, she fell in love with the cavapoo breed, a cross between a cavalier King Charles spaniel and a miniature poodle. She found a wonderful breeder and waited for the next litter of puppies to be born.

Emmie Mae is the love of her life. She is a kind, adorable, and funny dog who gives Ainsley unconditional love. She weighs eighteen pounds, her coat is a wavy light beige with reddish overtones, and she has big, inquisitive brown eyes. She covers all our faces with licks, especially Andrew's face. Ainsley is extremely responsible with her, taking her for long walks on trails every day, feeding her, and taking her to the vet. She held vigil with her after she was bitten by another dog last year, and they sleep side-by-side in bed. Emmie Mae centres Ainsley, and Ainsley has become more content with her own company and has been making better choices in life as a result. Ainsley tells everyone that Emmie Mae is the best thing that has ever happened to her.

In early 2021, Ainsley moved into a rental unit in Andrew's building. The children loved being one floor apart and cuddled with each other (and Emmie Mae, of course) every evening. Several months later, a lovely two-bedroom condo just five minutes away came on the market. We purchased it for Ainsley, knowing that the security of owning her own place is as important to her as it is for Andrew. The unit has sweeping views and is sunny and quiet, and the building has lots of dogs. I was initially fearful that she and Andrew would miss living in the same building, but they FaceTime each other every morning and every evening and see each other several times a week. Her condo is a magical place for her.

And Ainsley continues to excel at her job. The principals at the schools where she has worked have unfailingly complimented her and told her that she is able to help the most complex, vulnerable children. Of course she has difficult days, particularly when the children misbehave badly or become aggressive or when she disagrees with a colleague about what a child needs, but she is adept at standing her ground and being firm but fair. She is dedicated to her work and often spends after-school hours communicating back and forth with her co-workers and the children's parents.

Ainsley has purposely chosen not to disclose her disorders to her employers and co-workers. She has witnessed other people treat individuals with a mental health diagnosis differently and as "less" of a person. Misunderstandings, stigma, and misinformation can abound, and she wants, above all, to be treated like any other child and youth worker. Yet paradoxically, the empathy and deep understanding that she shows the children under her care and that are the hallmarks of her success come from her own lived experiences and challenges. She can more easily put herself in their shoes and help.

As a family, we moved our family doctor to the family practice team at our local hospital last year. It is a five-minute drive from our house, and I like the idea of being affiliated with a teaching hospital. The doctors there have been proactive and responsive, and Ainsley made the decision herself to transition her psychiatric care from Dr. Hamidi, whose practice has increasingly become focused on cannabis, to a consulting psychiatrist at the hospital who advises the family practice doctors. Dr. Hamidi was 100 per cent supportive and generously told Ainsley that she will always be there for her.

I love Ainsley's spirit and sense of adventure. She and Andrew and David took a train trip from Winnipeg to Jasper years ago so that David could show them the mountains and Western Canadian scenery. She and David have hiked through the rainforests of Costa Rica and have visited Barbados, where some of David's ancestors came from. She travelled to Australia with her high school class and to St. Lucia with a friend. She also had the opportunity to accompany David and me on some of my business trips to Turkey and Switzerland. As an adrenaline junkie, she loves rollercoasters and bungee jumping, and has done the EdgeWalk at the CN Tower.

David and I enjoy spending special time with Ainsley. We play board games like Boggle after dinner almost every evening, and she wins far too often! I sleep over at her condo most Friday nights, and we watch movies and giggle. She has reconnected with her former apartment-mate Sophie; they see each other on many weekends and go on long walks to lakes and trails with their dogs. And she has developed a valued friendship with another dog owner, whose mother, husband, and three children have welcomed her as part of their family. Nevertheless, she yearns for more friends her age. She still struggles to reach out to others socially, particularly her peers, and she continues to be overly sensitive to their comments. She carries ongoing fear that she will misunderstand their social cues and that they will misread what she says.

Additional challenges remain. She continues to experience episodes of deep anger that build inside her and frighten her. She knows that she will scare Emmie Mae if she screams or loses control in front of her; instead, she isolates herself, with her door closed, so that she can cry and hit her pillows to get her anger out. When she has largely calmed down, a long, tight bear hug (similar to a crisis intervention-type hug) really helps. Warm baths also consistently soothe her. Physically, she continues to suffer from intermittent nausea that appears to be related to her anxiety, as extensive physical tests have all been normal. She has tried different medications to attack the nausea, such as pantoprazole and Prevacid tablets, but none have helped. She has been more bothered by panic attacks recently. And she still grinds her teeth in her sleep so much that her jaws have again become increasingly sore.

Emotionally, Ainsley's deep-seated anxiety continues to interfere with her life and cause her significant distress. When she returned to the classroom with the Omicron variant raging, her eyes began ticking so much that she found it difficult to drive. She picks at her nail cuticles until they bleed. And her vocal tics have become more prevalent; they sound like retching, and she has been having trouble controlling them.

Ainsley's executive function and lack of organization skills also concern me. She is self-aware and knows she needs structure. But she continues to find it difficult to motivate herself to complete needed tasks and get things done, whether renewing her membership in her professional association, calling the pharmacy about her medications, or saving money to invest each month. I have to regularly remind her of these or she self-admittedly falls apart and feels worse about herself. She misses important appointments, including a recent virtual meeting with a doctor, and still cannot seem to keep up with cleaning her condo, shopping for necessities, or putting away her laundry. Every evening, we review her To Do list and I ask her to put them in her phone as reminders. We then go over them again the next morning; she is slowly improving but has a long road ahead. Her financial literacy is also limited, and, while she disagrees with me, budgeting is out of her grasp. She will always need support in these areas.

Ainsley is excellent, however, at remembering to take her medications and values their benefits. In response to those parents who have asked, her current prescriptions include these:

Strattera for ADD and anxiety: 50 mg
Neurontin for anxiety: 600 mg twice a day
Lamictal for mood stabilization: 100 mg twice a day
Clonazepam for mood and anxiety: 0.5 mg twice a day
Cipralex for mood and anxiety: 40 mg
Clonidine for ADD and anxiety: 0.2 mg

She also takes 85 mg of Suvexx for migraines and CBD oil for anxiety on an as-needed basis.

Ainsley recently decided that she needed to find a new psychologist. Through the Tourette Canada support group that David has co-led for years and in which she actively participates, she was introduced to MindFit Health, the same psychology clinic that Andrew was also referred to. She meets with one of their psychologists biweekly to focus on her anxiety, with another psychologist lined up to help her with her tics and executive function issues. She has been very pleased with the program thus far, which involves homework that exposes her to situations that induce her anxieties. She is eager to progress.

From a psychiatric point of view, the doctors at our local hospital were upfront with us that they are not equipped to deal with Tourette syndrome. Luckily, both she and Andrew have started to see the same highly respected Canadian neurodevelopmental psychiatrist.

Ainsley is well aware of her challenges and takes inspiration from Rachel Platten's "Fight Song." It helps empower her to keep fighting against her inner demons. I plan to give her the necklace that I wear with the word *STRONG* engraved on the locket. It perfectly describes who she is.

Ainsley has agreed to be Andrew's primary guardian for his personal care after David and I die. We have been extremely careful not to burden her with his caretaking at this point, and I know that she is terrified at times of the prospect of overseeing Andrew, much less taking care of herself. Nevertheless, she is responsible and excellent with him. He increasingly looks to her for advice on everything from understanding women to reminding him of the best strategies for grappling with an obsessive thought or ritual, like needing to reboot his computer multiple times. She is firm but fair with him, and they love, understand, and respect each other deeply. Although he remains concerned that she will become overwhelmed with this future responsibility, he is confident in her abilities and no longer asks me if she will be able to take care of him.

We have legally set up a team of three advisors to assist her — both with Andrew and with herself — after we die. She agrees that she will need significant help, especially with anything related to finances. We tell her that she must hire help whenever she needs it and that she doesn't have to do everything alone. Of course I worry about her future and am filled with heaviness at the thought of her having to take on the major responsibility for Andrew's caretaking in the future. But I know that she has successfully persevered through unbelievable challenges, and I am confident that she will continue to do so. She repeatedly tells me that while she is scared, she wouldn't have it any other way.

I am in awe of this beautiful young woman. She has faced insurmountable odds, finished university, and found a fulfilling career. She is my best friend.

part three

INSIGHTS

TELLING OUR STORY

This has not been an easy journey for David and me. Our lives have been turned inside out. We have bounced from despair and helplessness to hope and pride and back again. We have been through terrifying roller coaster rides experiencing Andrew's rages and rituals, impulsivity, anxiety, and neediness, and Ainsley's out-of-control behaviour and anxiety, physical aggression, and fragility. The journey to find psychiatrists and psychologists who are empathetic, supportive, and willing to work with us in true partnership, to find schools and educators who accommodate each child's unique needs in a holistic manner, and to find the right living accommodations for each child has been exhausting and exhilarating. We have been consumed with helping each child find their niche in life and prepare for the future. We have had to become comfortable living with a never-ending pattern of trial and error as natural consequences of dealing with these disorders. We have made many mistakes and have had many successes, and we know that the cycle is bound to continue.

I initially thought about writing this book as a catharsis for myself. But as I thought about it more, the idea of helping other parents who are experiencing similar challenges with their children resonated with me. I was also interested in educating families, friends, health care professionals, educators, and employers who deal with individuals with these disorders about the complex and often overwhelming issues that parents face. I strongly believe in giving back, and helping others is a core part of who I am. And as I look back, I know that David and I would have greatly benefited from a deeper understanding of what other families were experiencing, how they handled their crises, and what worked and didn't.

I firmly decided, however, that I wouldn't expose David, Andrew, and Ainsley to a wider audience unless they were unanimously supportive. Would they be comfortable with me hanging out our lives for the world to see? One Sunday family dinner, I broached the topic with them. David and Ainsley agreed to read the manuscript once I completed it and to give me their reactions, and I told Andrew that he and I would read it together since it would be too difficult for him to do alone.

After I finished my first draft, they each read it. All three of them insisted that I go forward, although they each voiced differing concerns. David is a much more private person than I am and was a bit unsettled about the idea of exposing our lives in detail and potentially stigmatizing the children in other people's eyes. Andrew was pleased but afraid that people would think badly of him after they read about some of the incidents that his impulsivity has driven him to do. Ainsley grappled with the fact that her employer will likely find out about her mental health challenges and learning disabilities and that people's opinions of her might change and affect their relationships. But they firmly agreed that they want our story told in the hopes that it can help other families facing similar situations. I was clear with each of them from the beginning that I would never publish one word that they did not want anyone else to read, and I have stuck by that promise. My family comes first.

WHAT WE'VE LEARNED

David and I had great hopes for the future as young parents. We had on rose-coloured glasses, neither of us ever having faced significant difficulties in our lives, and we assumed that our children's lives would fall into the same successful pattern as ours had. Raising two children with multiple mental health disorders came as a shock to us and sent us on a roller coaster of a journey that continues today. It has taught us important life lessons about parenting our children and about life in general. It has opened our worlds in a multitude of ways and has taught us to be better parents, partners, and individuals. These are the insights that I wish someone had gifted me as I started my journey.

Trust your gut as a parent

You know your child better than anyone else. If you think something is wrong, it generally is. It is obviously important to listen to parenting and health care experts, but if what they say doesn't resonate with you, keep looking.

David and I had to learn that most pediatricians, doctors, and even general psychologists are not trained and qualified to deal with complex mental health disorders. When Andrew was a baby and cried excessively, flapped his arms, and showed a lack of self-control when it came to food, we knew in our guts that something was wrong. We stayed up to all hours talking about it. We read a myriad of parenting books and consulted our doctor, but he kept telling us that we were overreacting. I remember leaving his office one time and feeling completely helpless, even questioning whether *I* was the problem as a AAA-type mother who just needed to relax. As new parents, we were inexperienced and didn't know what we were doing. The constant rebuffs perplexed me, made me despondent, and took their toll on my confidence. It was only after a few years — although it seemed like an eternity at the time — that I came to understand that our doctor was well-meaning but in no position to help us and hadn't even recognized the need to refer us earlier to appropriate specialists.

It is important to be tenacious. This does not mean being overly aggressive, but when I was not comfortable with what one professional told us, I learned to seek a second opinion. And a third if needed. When Ainsley was referred to a dialectical behaviour specialist and it quickly became apparent that the therapy was too rigid for her and did not fit her issues, I immediately put an end to those sessions and continued searching until we found Dr. Hamidi. And when Dr. Sherman's and Andrew's relationship became less productive after twenty fruitful years together, I didn't hesitate to contact as many health care professionals and parents as possible until I found a psychologist who both Andrew and I were confident could help him.

Parents in crisis must remember that they are not alone. David and I sought out support groups until we found the one that resonated with us. Shortly after attending the ADD parent support group in which no other child experienced rages, David read an article that linked Tourette syndrome with rages. We read voraciously about this disorder and started attending the local Tourette Canada support group. We knew we had found a home as we listened to the parents in the group. We shared nightmare stories about our children's rages and tics and tried to find humour in them. It was comforting to know that we were not the only parents who faced the issues we did. To this day, David and I find support groups reaffirming and helpful, reminding us of strategies that work for others and providing a community of individuals with empathetic, understanding ears facing similar challenges.

I have carried this lesson with me through my life. I insist on finding specialists who are qualified and experienced in Andrew and Ainsley's disorders. Don't settle for less. Look for those angels!

Talk openly with your children

Mental health disorders are terrifying for both children and their parents. Children are naturally frightened when they don't understand what is happening in their lives or why their behaviour is out of control. They can experience anguish and shame when they don't understand why they are causing such pain for their families and themselves. It's important for parents to be able to discuss their children's feelings with them, listen to them carefully, and let them know that their fears are understood and they are valued.

David and I realized early on that we needed to overcome our own hesitations and have open, transparent conversations with both Andrew and Ainsley, no matter how painful. It wasn't easy. We encouraged both children to share their feelings. When Andrew started having rages and told us that he didn't know why and just wanted to die, I froze inside. When Ainsley told us that the only way to get rid of the chaos inside herself was to act out, I shrunk inside myself. It was only by picking myself up and forcing myself to shake off these feelings that I was able to overcome these instinctual reactions.

After reading the note Ainsley left on my bed in which she described her distress with her anxiety and misbehaviour, I moved quickly to talk with her about her fears. This validated her feelings and showed her that I was on her side and not afraid to discuss the elephant in the room. We let the children know they were not "bad," that instead it was their disorders causing havoc, and that we understood what they were feeling and would help.

And we didn't shy away from discussing the children's medications with them. Some parents have told me they fear their children won't want to take medications and so instead tell them that they are taking special vitamins. I don't believe this is helpful. Our children both desperately wanted help for their problems. We involved them in their own treatment and educated them about what each medication was used for. We asked them how they felt in order to monitor side effects and hopeful improvements, particularly when changes or new medications were introduced. As they became older, this empowered them to become increasingly active in their own treatment.

We also were careful, especially in the early days, to pay extra attention to Ainsley as Andrew's sibling. Even though we had to spend enormous time with him, we knew that Ainsley was deeply affected by his rages and we didn't want her to unwittingly become relegated to second-tier status. In addition to sending her to the urban farm's program for siblings experiencing trauma, we spent extra time alone with her at home, whether playing Candyland or baking together. We openly discussed Andrew's challenges with her at her level, which greatly helped her understand what was happening in both their lives and further validated her feelings.

By talking openly with them, we gave our children the confidence to know that we had heard them, that we understood and valued their feelings and fears, and that, through this understanding, we would find the right help for them. Good parenting is all about good communication.

Research, research, research

Embrace the power of research. Knowledge is key to understanding, finding the right resources, and being an effective advocate.

I conducted much of my initial research before the Internet had developed to the extent it is today. I read everything that I could, spent days in libraries, and made call after call, talking with as many professionals, associations, and parents as possible. I participated in support groups and refused to settle until my gut (there's that word again!) told me that I had done what I could. Reading *The Boy Who Couldn't Stop Washing* gave me the framework to understand Andrew's OCD and how to deal with it. Speaking with parents of children with Tourette syndrome helped me learn how to handle tics and rages. It was overwhelming at times to try to identify the right help. But it is important to persevere until you find the answers you're looking for.

Of course the thing about research is that it can be never-ending. I had to recognize when I had done my best and the law of diminishing returns was kicking in. I had to learn to stop and breathe.

My research has never been complete. As Andrew and Ainsley grew, new findings, medications, therapies, and treatments emerged. I did my best to stay current to keep educating myself. It didn't require the same breadth and intensity as my initial research, unless new critical information came up. I still regularly seek the latest information on their disorders. And I make sure to target each child's specific needs, whether determining the most effective job accommodations for Andrew or finding a family doctor for Ainsley who can empathize with her so that she doesn't shut down.

Not all of my early research was focused on the children's special needs. General parenting best practices also applied. As I found out after putting Ainsley in ballet and Brownies, she was much happier participating in activities she was interested in, not the ones I wanted for her. The same went for finding the right school placements: just because a parent attended a prestigious school doesn't mean her daughter should. I tried to become child-centred and listen to what my children were saying and wanted.

An essential part of my research has always involved looking into the benefits and risks of each medication that the children's doctors prescribe. I ask about the risks and long-term side effects. Some of the medications, particularly stimulants, can cause eating and sleeping problems. Other medications, like the antipsychotics Risperdal and Abilify, can cause increased appetite with rapid and significant weight gain. Both Andrew and Ainsley experienced this. And others can be addictive, as Ainsley found with clonazepam with its debilitating physical withdrawal effects. Parents have a responsibility to understand their children's medications, weigh the risks against the benefits, and observe changes in their behaviour.

I have also learned that although the Internet is a crucial source of research, it is important to verify the information with experts and learn what to ignore. The dire stories and warnings that some people write, as well as the promotion of certain alternative treatments and diets, can be both alluring and scary. I am a strong believer in trying anything that may help my children, but a number of "treatments" espoused on the Internet not only make no sense to me but can be harmful, at least to my children. For example, there is a group of parents and professionals who advocate that medications should *not* be given to autistic children and that they can be "cured" in other ways. Some believe that the incidence of autism is linked to vaccines. Others espouse that autism can be caused by mercury exposure and promote alternative therapies such as chelation therapy, which involves injecting a patient with a synthetic chemical to rid the body of toxins. The medical and scientific articles that I have read and the professionals with whom I have spoken have consistently disputed any link between these claims and autism. They note that a few of these therapies can even lead to dangerous side effects, like kidney damage. Autism cannot be cured.

Keep digging for information that can help. Remember that knowledge is power: research not only broadens our understanding of the complexities of these disorders and potential treatment options, but it allows parents to make more informed decisions about their children's care. Persevere. Be relentless.

Embrace needed medications and therapy

I am a strong proponent that medications and therapy go hand in hand. They are powerful partners that help one another. In mild cases, I have seen either therapy or medication alone be effective. In many other cases, however — like both Andrew's and Ainsley's — medications are needed first to sufficiently change the brain's chemistry before therapy can be effective.

I recognize that many parents are understandably wary of taking a pharmacological approach to treatment, not only because of potential physical damage to their children's bodies but because of the fear of stigma they may face in the community. David and I, however, have never had any such concerns: people living with diabetes and epilepsy take widely approved medications, and we view the brain as just another part of the body. The children's medications attack the chemical imbalances in their brains to facilitate improved functioning. Yes, there are side effects and delicate interactions between the medications that must be carefully monitored and weighed. The children undergo regular blood tests and electrocardiograms to check that their organs and tissues continue to be healthy. But I believe Andrew would be institutionalized without his medications. Risperdal stopped his rages in their tracks. Luvox and Anafranil have lessened his OCD. Ainsley would be wild and out of control without Strattera, Neurontin, and Lamictal. For us, the benefits of these medications have greatly outweighed any risks.

Many teenagers refuse to take medications, often because it makes them "different" from their peers. Fortunately, neither Andrew nor Ainsley has ever challenged taking them. They have been part of their lives from an early age. Both children swallow their medications in one gulp both at breakfast and at dinner, and they are fully aware of how critical they have been — and continue to be — for their functioning. Ainsley recently forgot to take her morning medications and told me that she felt out of sorts and more unfocused than she should have been that day. Andrew thanks Dr. Biederman at every visit for prescribing Anafranil a few years ago to better fight and control his OCD.

As our children grew, diagnostic changes occurred. Andrew was initially diagnosed with OCD, but then diagnoses of Tourette syndrome and ADD were added. Many families have told us that they were jarred or upset by new or changing diagnoses, as they were unprepared for new criteria that affect major decisions on their children's medications, therapy, education, and the like. David and I never sought to place labels on our children, but we were not afraid of them as we understood that proper diagnoses are critical in creating the most effective treatment plans. Some parents may prefer to discuss their child's behaviours versus using the names of their disorders. For us, diagnoses have been useful in everything from helping to classify Andrew as "exceptional" in order to obtain special education placement to finding the right psychologists for Ainsley.

Sometimes a change in psychiatrist and/or therapist is warranted. We are indebted to Dr. Sherman, who played such an instrumental role helping Andrew learn to control his OCD, anxiety, and impulsivity for years until they outgrew one another. Ainsley experienced a similar transition when her psychiatrist, Dr. Hamidi, transitioned her practice to more of a cannabis focus. It is obviously scary to make the change, but it is not necessarily negative or damaging.

Medications and therapy involve trial and error. Some will help your children enormously while others will not work. Don't be afraid to make mistakes on the path to finding effective medications and specialists. And don't give up!

Insist on an integrated partnership approach

When it comes to care, I strongly believe in the maxim that the whole is greater than the sum of its parts. The best outcomes occur when all caregivers are on the same page about a child's treatment plan, and when the people involved in this care share information and listen to each other's perspectives.

Andrew and Ainsley have benefited from this approach in spades. Dr. Sherman's observations about Andrew's behaviour to Dr. Biederman helped Dr. Biederman decide which medications to prescribe. Montcrest School's partnership with Dr. Paris and us allowed them to implement strategies customized to help Ainsley succeed, whether giving her more breaks or helping her chunk her work. Being able to communicate with the school about how each child's weekend or previous evening had been ensured that their teachers understood what was happening in their lives. One afternoon, Douglas Academy let me know that Andrew had fallen asleep for two hours in class; they were not concerned, because I had informed them that he had just started the powerful medication Risperdal that stopped his rages, and his body was simply adjusting to it.

Ainsley would have undoubtedly been thrown out of numerous classrooms had her principals, teachers, Dr. Paris, and we as her parents not met regularly to plan a coordinated approach. Yes, certain initiatives didn't work: when told to go into the hall, Ainsley didn't see it as a consequence but as a relief and simply wandered. This led the school to implement different consequences, such as having a staff member sit with her outside the classroom.

The contrast between Andrew's employment with the police and his employment with Rogers also points to the importance of this teamwork. The police meant well, but Rogers put that well-meaning into action by treating David and me as true partners in Andrew's success in the workplace. They listened to the information I shared with them, brought in a job coach, implemented accommodations like fixed hours, and provided Andrew with a special mentor. They call me whenever a minor issue bubbles up, such as Andrew being distracted at work, so that we can deal with it before it mushrooms into a larger issue. They even share future career thinking with me, and they have respected my advice that career *enhancement* versus career *advancement* is the key for Andrew at this time to best control his anxiety and allow him to flourish.

To this day, I follow one rule: if a professional has no interest in involving David and me and my children's core caretakers as a team, it's time to move to someone else.

Reset your expectations for your life

Caring for children with serious mental health disorders often means that life will not be able to continue as planned or hoped for. These disorders affect the entire family and throw each family member's life into disarray. Fear, anger, and resentment will bubble to the surface at times. That's okay. Accepting this is key to being able to move forward.

David and I started our journeys as young parents with hopes and dreams of happy, successful children who would excel at school, in sports, and socially; who would enjoy travelling and exploring the world; and who would mature into loving, responsible adults who might even take care of us in our old age. We dreamed of going on family vacations and maintaining strong relationships with friends and our families.

Yet the reality of our situation couldn't have been more different. We were terrified of Andrew's rages and bizarre rituals and of Ainsley's out-of-control behaviour and paralyzing anxieties. And while we were moving forward with diagnoses and different treatments, we stopped having any social life. We could not have friends over for fear that Andrew would have a rage or that Ainsley would misbehave or become physically aggressive. Similarly, we could not go out to friends' homes together or meet them at restaurants, as we needed a professionally trained sitter. Our nanny was exhausted in the evenings and needed breaks. And no agencies would send anyone to stay with our children given their profiles. Friends were initially sympathetic, but they lacked experience with mental illness and often feared it. This affected David more than me: although he is an introvert at heart, he is naturally more social than I am, and he missed the large number of social interactions he had previously enjoyed.

David and I had to learn early on to rely largely on ourselves. This was compounded by the fact that neither of us had family in Toronto. But we were not afraid to reach out for help. It was unfortunate that the psychologist from whom we sought parenting advice was not helpful, but that did not stop me from connecting with other medical professionals, parent support groups, and other parents of special-needs children. Sometimes just having a sympathetic ear, like Andrew's friend Duncan's parents, is enough. But when more intensive support is needed, it is important not to ignore the need.

Revise your thinking about your own lives. Learn to accept the reality of your family situation and enjoy whatever happiness comes your way. Embrace every win.

Recalibrate your expectations of family

Your expectations for your own life and for your children's futures aren't the only things that will change after your child is diagnosed with a mental health disorder. Relationships with family will likely change as well.

When our children were young, David and I found that our well-meaning family members often didn't understand what we were experiencing. I remember how puzzled David's family was by our horror and concern as Andrew ate piece after piece of his birthday cake. I remember my deep distress when my mother told me not to let Andrew get fat on Risperdal and to be stricter with Ainsley to turn around her unruly behaviour. I felt like I had lost my best friend.

Many parents have told us that their families are too busy with their own lives to help. Others have come to the painful conclusion that their relatives are not interested in becoming involved in the complex challenges facing their children. Some have discussed their relatives' erroneous impressions about mental illness, believing that their children are contagious, morally deficient, or a stain on the family name. Still others have commented on their own mothers' or fathers' fear of the unknown.

While we were raising our kids, David and I desperately needed respite. But with all our family members living hours away, their physical assistance was limited. They checked in with us, provided sympathetic ears, and visited when they could. David's sister even flew each of the children to her home in Ottawa for fun weekends. Holidays with family sounded idyllic in principle but often turned into exhausting vacations for us, with Andrew performing non-stop rituals and Ainsley climbing over everything, not listening to directions, and generally being out of control. The children were in constant emotional and physical turmoil.

Aside from my mother's comments about Ainsley's misbehaviour and Andrew's weight, she was the family member who provided me with the greatest comfort. She spent an inordinate amount of time on the phone with both children — every day — and really listened to them. A few years before she died, I remember how hard she laughed after she told Andrew that she needed a new crown on one tooth; he matter-of-factly pointed out that, at age eighty-five, it would be foolish to spend money on a new crown because she would likely die soon! She delighted in repeating this story to everyone. And as Ainsley blossomed, my mother celebrated her successes and encouraged her to keep reaching for her goals. I was particularly touched when she told Ainsley that she deserved to be happy. Like me, my mother was a physical hugger and kisser, and she enveloped both children in love. Her actions bolstered me when I needed it most.

In 2015, at the age of eighty-nine, my mother entered palliative care, having suffered from painful irritable bowel disease, ulcerative colitis, and diverticulitis for years. I thought my heart would break. Shortly before she died, I whispered how much I loved her and thanked her for everything she had done for the children and for me. Her death has left an unfillable hole in my life.

Yes, blood is thicker than water, but in the case of families living with children with mental health disorders, blood can falter. Understanding and accepting family members' behaviour doesn't mean they don't love you. Make peace with them and be thankful for the support you receive.

Be prepared that friends may not provide the support you want or need

With mental illness comes stigma. A lack of understanding can cause fear. Some friends may distance themselves instead of providing needed support. Other friends will stay close, but having a child with these disorders will likely require you to adapt your friendships. And you may find that you need different types of friendships than you once had to ensure you have the support you need.

David and I were very hurt when Andrew's friend's parents suddenly pulled him from their friendship. One of my friends simply disappeared from my life after I discussed my distress with the children's behaviours, even though I had actively supported her during her own daughter's hospitalization a few years before. I realized how lucky I was to have a supportive spouse, something that many parents with special-needs children don't have.

David is far more understanding of friends than I am. He is reluctant to prevail upon them and has never been inclined to ask for support. He feels that they have their own busy lives. Especially when the children were young, he didn't openly share many details of the challenges we were facing other than to let them know that we were dealing with family mental health issues. However, he never misses a chance to extoll the children's successful achievements. He would rather promote the positive side of their lives than dwell on their challenges.

I have always wanted and needed friends' support. I am much more of an open book than David. My best friend from university has two special-needs children of her own and has always been supportive of me, as I have of her, but most of my friendships faded as the children's challenges became all-consuming. This was compounded by the fact that as their issues drained my energy, I lacked the reserves to invest in developing and maintaining friendships of my own.

David and I discovered that we often obtain the most support from other parents of children with mental health challenges. They implicitly understand the complexities of dealing with children like ours and the stressors we face in our lives. Together, we can laugh at stories that other parents would find alarming, whether Andrew's impulsivity causing inappropriate behaviour with computers, Ainsley's rude swearing at her teachers, or Andrew's risk-taking friend Duncan hanging out of his bedroom window on the second floor of his home. We can also support and comfort one another when times are particularly tough. Just having an understanding ear who listens and commiserates, who provides needed advice, and who cheers you up is often enough.

Seek out friendships that are supportive. Don't spend time brooding over the loss of those who do not provide you with what you need. Life is short, and parents of special-needs children lack the emotional cushion to devote to anyone who isn't a true friend.

Be kind to your spouse/partner

Children's mental health disorders play havoc with marriages and partnerships. True partnership means reaching informed decisions together about your children's treatment, education, and housing; participating equally in their care; and providing each other with essential emotional support. This requires a lot of trust and giving your partner the benefit of the doubt.

David and I are fortunate to have survived as a couple. Many couples don't. The strain can be debilitating. We have witnessed parents blame one another for their child's problems. We have participated in support groups where one spouse has accused the other of having a lack of interest in their child. We have overheard disagreements about how to handle everything from diagnoses and discipline to medications and therapy. Medications, in particular, can be a major source of conflict, as one parent may either not believe in the need for medication or fear that the medication will turn their child into a "zombie." We have listened to spouses undermine one another's decisions. These factors can understandably divide spouses and heighten the risk of divorce. Separation and divorce, in turn, lead to further complications for both the children and themselves.

David and I have not been totally immune from these issues. The demands of Andrew's and Ainsley's care have been so overwhelming at times as to leave no time for each other. Yet we have always understood the critical importance of trusting one another and leaning on each other. Early on, we learned to joke about the genesis of the children's disorders: David has a restless leg that jumps up and down when he's seated, which can be a sign of ADD. He has a relative who repetitively eye-blinks and shrugs whenever we see him. And my family clearly has perfectionist and obsessive tendencies. But it doesn't really matter where these disorders come from, although it is interesting and important from research and clinical points of view. What matters is that we act harmoniously in our children's best interests and try to carve out satisfying lives as spouses.

David and I balance each other: he calms me down, and I instill more urgency in him. I conduct the great majority of the research, finding doctors, schools, and housing and interacting with Andrew's employers. David has played a vital role as the fun parent, going to baseball and hockey games with the children, helping to coach many of their childhood teams, and taking them camping. Of course we have had disagreements through the years: he isn't comfortable with conflict, and I wish that he was firmer, less accommodating, and more decisive. His slowness to respond to issues (at least in relation to my pace) can drive me mad. His hands-off approach and refusal to become involved with disagreements that I have with the children — particularly ones that we have discussed, such as admonishing Ainsley after she has been disrespectful to me or deciding whether Andrew should be allowed to purchase a new phone — upset me. In turn, he rightfully sees me as rigid, too direct, and overly decisive. He has not had to do much of the heavy lifting, not because of any unwillingness on his part but because I am internally wired to take charge; he himself looks back with surprise at his somewhat laissez-faire attitude in the early days when he hoped the children wouldn't need extensive intervention and that their struggles would work themselves out. He knows that he needed me to find the right help. And he has been my rock. Dr. Sherman held several sessions with us to help determine how best to handle situations in a coordinated fashion. It still isn't easy.

Through it all, we have worked to maintain open communication with one another and the commitment to move forward together. We believe in and respect one another. We try to remember to be kind. We keep a close eye on any tendency to accuse or blame each other. And we hold on tight to one another.

Take care of yourself

It seems obvious to say, but it is important to stay healthy. Healthy people have more energy, can better control stress, generally feel good about themselves, and are better able to build reserves to deal with difficulties in their lives. If you are not healthy, you cannot take care of your children, much less yourself, particularly when your children are in crisis.

I have never been afraid to reach out to obtain the support I need, whether to a psychologist, support groups, or other parents. There is nothing wrong — and so much to gain — in getting help when I need it, not only as a parent but as an individual. Focusing on my own health has allowed me to deal with issues on my mind and come to peace with many of them. By doing so, my emotional fortitude has grown stronger, giving me the room to focus on Andrew and Ainsley.

I sometimes think back to my early meeting with the psychologist who told me that I couldn't "have it all." Although he didn't have any real understanding of our lives, he was right in one domain — my health. I know that I am strong and resilient. I excelled at my high-pressure job and relentlessly persevered through the devastating challenges at home, but something had to give. I have always been thin and have kept up with fitness, but my eating became unhealthy, either skipping meals or grabbing ice cream and candy to get me through each day. I am convinced that my eating, combined with all the stresses and pressures in my life, undoubtedly contributed not only to my cancer diagnosis but to my additional health problems, which have included ongoing kidney problems, high blood pressure, osteoporosis, and long-term back problems.

Rightly or wrongly, I have never viewed any of my medical conditions, with the exception of cancer, as major events in my life. Perhaps it is unhealthy to minimize them, but I have always taken the attitude of obtaining the needed treatment or surgery and moving on with my life. David is understandably concerned with my cavalier attitude. I sometimes half-joke that if stress is a major determinant of stroke, I should have died years ago. I have seen a number of nutritional and health care professionals and know what I must do to change; I am trying my best — for example, assiduously drinking two and a half litres of water each day and following a Mediterranean diet, but it is not natural for me.

Part of taking care of my health is being cognizant of my surroundings. This is not one of my strengths. In 2021, I suffered multiple wrist fractures while hiking with Ainsley and Emmie Mae after I flew over a tree stump. Several months later, I gashed my leg when I tripped over the open door of Andrew's dishwasher and needed stitches. And then I broke a toe after stubbing it on a chair. One of our neighbours has suggested that I cover myself in bubble wrap. I feel like the Energizer bunny who just keeps going, but I know that I must stop rushing around and be more careful.

We all know that in addition to eating healthfully, getting enough sleep and exercising regularly are beneficial. Sleep has fortunately never been an issue for me. Only when one of the children is in crisis do my nights become interrupted as I lie in bed, worrying and plotting how to bring them out of their misery. David unfortunately is not a good sleeper and continues to try numerous strategies to attack this problem, like reading if he wakes up in the middle of the night.

David and I both enjoy exercise. He swims every week, skis during the winter, and plays golf in the warmer months, although he recently claimed that his golf game hasn't improved since he was twelve years old. Fitness has been always important to both my physical and emotional health. I enjoy working out in the gym and find that my time on the treadmill is instrumental in allowing me to think through my problems. I have also started aquafit classes three times a week, even though the thought of getting in the pool during the cold winter months gives me shivers.

Humour has been an important ingredient in my and my family's coping toolkit. As Ainsley recently reminded me, if we don't laugh we will cry. We chuckled at Andrew when one of his teachers told him that some school rules were set in stone and he literally asked, "And where is the stone kept?" We giggle at Ainsley's uncanny ability to make up words each evening during our Boggle games that are accepted as valid by the Scrabble dictionary. We find it important to poke fun at our lives together and not always take them too seriously.

And, as hard as it is sometimes, I try to be kind to myself. I quietly compliment myself on my strength and perseverance. I also try to forgive myself for my mistakes, like having put Ainsley in that horrific situation of having to run outside in her nightgown during one of Andrew's rages. It's no easy task.

David and I have found it important to carve out parts of our lives as our own, not dedicated to the children or to each other. While everyone can benefit from the occasional distance from their partner, this is critical for parents of special-needs children. We can all too easily get lost in the morass of our children's struggles. When I don't take time for myself, I find myself run down and have faced the risk of burnout. Being alone allows me to regain perspective on the issues that David and I face together. Going for a walk, taking a bath, watching a movie by myself, or playing bridge helps me refuel and rebuild my own identity. David finds the same with golf, skiing, and swimming.

Don't forget the importance of respite

Respite is an essential part of taking care of yourself. It is a need, not just a want. Respite provides critical relief away from the challenges at home. It can take the form of hobbies, sports, work, or vacations. It also involves self-care, whether getting your hair done, nails manicured, or booking relaxing massages.

Respite has played a major role in my life, helping me to reduce stress and regain some sense of normalcy. Once both children were at Eagle Hill, David and I knew that we needed to do something for ourselves. We started taking duplicate bridge lessons, and I quickly became addicted. For me, bridge is more than an intriguing game. It gives me solace from the troubles in my life, whether related to the children, my work, or anything else, and forces me to fully focus on and "lose myself" in the game for three hours every time I play. Not only have I progressed quickly, attaining the rank of Diamond Life Master in 2021, but I have developed meaningful friendships with other players. They have essentially become my second family.

In addition, I developed an interest in genealogy shortly after my mother died. I joined Ancestry.com and have greatly enjoyed the sleuthing involved in identifying ancestors and connecting with newfound family members across the United States. I find it particularly exciting to make a new find — for example, building out an entirely new branch of the family with one of my maternal cousins.

My career also provided me with a critical outlet and sense of satisfaction and reward, as well as the income to pay for the children's medication and therapies that weren't covered by insurance. My job was one of the few places I could separate myself from the children and focus on other matters, even though I often had to be hyper-focused just to get through the day. I thrived in executive search. I became one of the firm's first female partners worldwide, became managing partner of the Toronto office, and was even named a member of the Global Executive Committee for several years. I placed hundreds of executives in chief executive officer and C-suite positions and on boards of directors for almost twenty-five years. My valued executive assistant, with whom I worked closely for over twenty years, unfailingly supported me. She protected me when I was upset and gave me room to grieve behind my closed office door or go for a walk. And she knew to interrupt me at any time if either child needed me.

David has also focused more on himself, although he emotionally needs less "alone" time away from the children than I do. He is gradually moving toward retirement, but he enjoys his work as a financial planner and particularly appreciates the ability to work from home post-COVID. He loves to putter in the house. He has taken numerous golf and ski trips with his friends, and he hopes to travel more in the future. He especially enjoys unwinding at the cottage in Quebec, where he can play golf, swim, and canoe in the summers and go cross-country skiing in the winters. It is a place where he can relax and catch up with childhood friends.

Parents of special-needs children must actively seek respite to lessen the stress in their daily lives caused by their children's disorders. It is not always possible to do so, but once a crisis lifts, take time for yourself. You have earned the right to enjoy some breathing room.

Make a financial plan

Raising special-needs children is expensive. Costs can include medications, therapy, and potentially having to support your children into adulthood, at which time you may have to cover education, housing, support workers, food, clothes, and transportation. Financial planning is critical in helping to navigate the potentially exorbitant costs that mental health disorders often involve. It helps protect a child's financial future and decrease risks from uncertainties and unplanned events.

David and I realize how fortunate we are to be able to provide for the children. The children's psychologists charge over $200 per session, and our provincial government-funded health insurance plan doesn't cover Dr. Biederman's or private psychology costs. Eagle Hill added to our financial burden, in U.S. dollars no less, as did Andrew's former private group home, each of which cost tens of thousands of dollars per year. And with Andrew incapable of caring for himself as an adult, we need to be able to provide for him for the future, including over the long term after David and I die. Ainsley needs our financial help with her biweekly therapy sessions, medical Botox injections, and veterinary costs.

Our stable and well-paying jobs have made these costs bearable. We have also had to make sacrifices. We don't have a second car, take expensive vacations, or spend needlessly. We will not have the freedom to leave Toronto once we both retire and spend extended time away, either travelling or in the sun. We have made these decisions so that we could provide Andrew and Ainsley with the best care and education we could and ensure that they each own a condo, which will provide them with a stable living situation in the years to come. David's expertise as a financial planner has meant that we have been able to put together the financial plans we need to secure our and our children's futures. We regularly review and update our wills and Andrew's guardianship documents.

I am acutely aware that many families face far more challenging financial situations. Canada does provide some economic help to families in need. In Ontario, for example, the Ontario Disability Support Program provides income and employment support to people with disabilities, and the Trillium Drug Program helps Ontario residents lower the cost of expensive prescription medications. But for many families it is still not enough to make ends meet. Navigating the system is extremely difficult and confusing, and takes up significant time. And time is a luxury that parents in crisis don't have.

Try to find a financial planner who is willing to collaborate with you to make a plan that responds to your family's and your children's particular situation. It can make the difference between having a secure future and an uncertain outcome.

Advocate and volunteer

Parents of special-needs children can play a critical role in influencing policy directions on mental health. Advocating and volunteering can help ensure that our children's rights receive the needed attention, that our voices are heard, and that we can have a meaningful impact on our government's health care decisions. Not every parent can find the strength nor the time to do so, especially when in crisis. But it is so beneficial to become involved, and it is personally uplifting to see the differences we can make in our children's lives.

Through our own journeys, both David and I have come to understand the importance of these activities. We have each joined different non-profit boards and have led various support groups. My advocacy work has included serving on the board of directors of Canada's largest psychiatric hospital and co-founding SickKids Hospital's parent advisory group on OCD. I participated on Dr. Biederman's parent advisory council for a number of years and have served on additional mental health boards, including currently chairing the board at Kerry's Place Autism Services, Canada's largest service provider for those with autism and their families.

David has been active with Tourette Canada's Toronto chapter and has co-led their monthly support group meetings for over twenty years. He sits on the board of an organization that helps find supportive housing for people with intellectual disabilities. He also volunteers with organizations that are not related to the children — for example, serving on the board of our local residents' association.

We are both committed to helping parents who are looking for guidance. We often take calls from those seeking help on matters such as how to find the right medical professionals, treatments, schools, and housing for their children, and how to approach the guardianship process.

We strongly believe in giving back and paying it forward, as well as in educating others about mental health disorders. We see it as our calling. If these disorders remain hidden from discussion, misunderstandings grow and we cannot move forward. As a family, we shout out about these conditions to help people understand there is nothing to be afraid of and that these disorders are chemical imbalances of the brain, similar to diseases in other parts of the body. Stigma is insidious. Education is key not only to informing others but also to minimizing the unfair judgments and unjust treatments of those with mental health disorders. That's why we agreed to participate in the documentary *OCD: The War Inside* years ago. Twenty years later, Andrew continues to receive thankful messages on social media from people around the world with OCD after they have watched his story on YouTube.

Both Andrew and Ainsley have joined David and me in volunteer work. Andrew has sat on panels about OCD and autism. He is active in Rogers's inclusion and diversity initiatives and participated in a Ready, Willing and Able training presentation about autism for a global company last year. Ainsley's speech about anxiety to the entire school at Montcrest led a number of her peers to thank her for speaking out about her struggles and educating them. She also actively participates in the Toronto Tourette Canada support group. Both of them raise funds and participate in an annual walk to increase awareness about autism. They are articulate mental health ambassadors and advocates.

I believe that we have been placed on this earth for a reason. For parents of children with challenges, I cannot think of a more worthwhile activity than to give back to our communities and move the mental health agenda forward. Repay the angels in your lives and get out there!

THE RIDE CONTINUES

Our family has been on a non-stop roller coaster ride since the children were born. The journey has been exhausting, disheartening, frustrating, and terrifying. It has equally been inspirational, educational, and eye-opening. I approach the world in a much more empathetic and less judgmental manner than I did when I was younger. Our journey has made me who I am today.

There have been times when I have quietly asked myself, "Why me? Why us?" and have become numb and despondent about my own future. I am not a religious person, but I have gone to church to pray. There was even a period when I didn't care if I died as I saw no happiness ahead: I ignored my health, didn't bother taking needed medications or seek treatment.

David has also been discouraged at times. It shook him when he realized that the children's behaviours were actually disorders with names, and it saddens him that they face a lifetime of challenges with more limited, sheltered lives than those of our friends' children. He sometimes bemoans the children's lack of independence and number of friends. But then he recalibrates and looks to their strengths and successes. He remembers Andrew animatedly debating the strength of the Toronto Blue Jays with a couple at a restaurant during one of the Jays' spring training sessions, and finding out a few nights later that the couple had returned the following evening hoping to see Andrew again. He recalls Ainsley's wonderful sense of adventure, appreciation for nature, and her joy at seeing the monkeys and crocodiles in Costa Rica. He remembers that Andrew has a wonderful full-time job, is able to get himself to and from work, and adores living in his condo. And he reminds himself that Ainsley is gifted at her full-time job, extremely caring and responsible with others, and the most loving dog owner. We are so proud that both children have found niches that make them happy.

Many people have tried to be gracious and have told us that our children are a special gift. I have heard this cliché on TV and have read it in numerous articles. It's utter garbage in my view. There is no question that our children are special. Yes, their issues have made me more understanding and have propelled me to become involved in advocacy and outreach. Yes, they have exposed me to new worlds of which I was ignorant and have made me more sensitive to people's challenges in life. But both children face serious, sometimes heartbreaking, issues every day. Their fight never ends. Who would want their children to have to continually negotiate adversity? Who would want them to continually suffer throughout their lives?

I still have days when I am so exhausted, so drained of energy, that all I want to do is curl up in a hole and disappear. In the worst of times, I feel like someone has punched me in the stomach, and, just as I am about to get up, another swing comes at me hard. In better times, my life is a constant vigil in which I am always on guard, holding my breath and trying not to wait for the next crisis. There is little relaxation. I have learned to try to enjoy the good times, knowing that they won't last, and to equally remind myself during the bad times that they, too, will lift.

Through all this, neither David nor I have ever regretted having the children, not for one second. We love Andrew and Ainsley deeply and want the very best lives for them as possible. We are fortunate in many ways and celebrate their successes. It took me years but I now realize that we can and do have fulfilling lives, just different than the ones I had envisioned.

Andrew recently told me that Ainsley lifts his spirits and gives him hope that his finest days are yet to come. It is wonderful to see the children act as each other's best support, but I worry about both of them, particularly and perhaps more surprisingly about Ainsley. Although she is more capable in many ways than Andrew, she is also more complex. I worry not only about the burden that will be placed on her having to care for Andrew in the future but how she will cope, given her own challenges with anxiety and organizing her own life, much less Andrew's.

But I also have great hopes and wishes for their futures. Of course I want them to be happy and stable. I want them to know that their perseverance and will to succeed will help them climb out of every crisis they face. I want them to be productive citizens who enjoy their jobs, give back to their communities, and engage in activities that give them joy, whether watching the Jays play or taking Emmie Mae for a long walk. I want them to remember that they are surrounded by people who love and support them. And I want them to understand how special they are and that they both make a difference in the lives of every person they touch.

In my wallet, I carry a laminated copy of the lyrics to "Everything's Alright" from the musical *Jesus Christ Superstar*. I take it out and reread it whenever I become stressed. It gives me perspective and reminds me to try not to worry.

Back in 2008, when the children were twenty-one and nineteen, Dr. Biederman asked each of them to address the Fifth Annual Pediatric Psychopharmacology Advisory Council hosted by the Department of Psychiatry at Mass General Hospital. They couldn't have been more excited. Both children wrote their own moving speeches. David flew with them to Boston to attend the event, which was packed with medical and health care professionals. Andrew spoke first, and the audience seemed to understand his every word, even with his speech impediment. He said that he "would much rather have cancer and have my life on the line due to the cancer than live through what I went through. It really was the definition of Hell.... Without Dr. Biederman, it would be safe to say that I would be dead today. He saved my life." Ainsley echoed similar sentiments, profusely thanking Dr. Biederman and saying, "Everyone deserves a chance at life. Everyone has something amazing to contribute to this world and you can't give up on them. You will make a difference in their life, whether you know it or not. Never give up."

Each day brings new challenges. When I was undergoing my cancer treatment, many people told me how brave I was. I always understood that this just was not true: I knew that my treatment journey would last one year and that then I would recover, while both Andrew and Ainsley are slated to face challenges every day of their lives. My children have successfully struggled against breathtaking adversity, have kept up their determination, and face life head on. I am in awe of them. They are my heroes.

ACKNOWLEDGEMENTS

Andrew's and Ainsley's angels have played extraordinary roles in our lives. They have helped the children, as well as David and me, overcome unrelenting adversity and learn to embrace life.

To our medical angels:

- Dr. Joseph Biederman, who inspires me every day with his unparallelled expertise, empathy, and caring
- Dr. Katharina Manassis, who started Andrew on his journey of discovery and recovery
- Dr. Till Davy, whose hugs lifted our spirits and kept us going when we thought we couldn't
- Dr. Jeffrey Sherman, who so adeptly guided Andrew through the minefields of his youth, as well as kindly paying for all those meals together
- Dr. Pamela Paris, who stuck by Ainsley throughout her difficult youth and oversaw her transformation into an amazing young adult
- Dr. Jinous Hamidi, who, in Ainsley's words, saved her life
- Dr. Paul Sandor, whose quiet amusement at Andrew provided me with needed perspective and solace
- Dr. Kim Edwards, Dr. Laura Katz, and the team at MindFit Health for recently taking on Andrew and Ainsley
- Dr. Elia Abi-Jaoude, our newest angel

205

To our academic angels:

- Nora McKay at Bedford Park School, who got us through the worst year of Andrew's life with her empathy and understanding
- Colleen Bacon Forrest and her wonderful teachers at the Douglas Academy, who guided Andrew from Grades 4 to 8 with invaluable instruction and emotional support, giving him the confidence to succeed
- Elaine Danson and her caring team at Montcrest School, especially Erene Augustyn, Terry Sherrard, Kim McCallum, Dan Bailey, and Billy Brown, all of whom endured Ainsley's out-of-control behaviours with compassion, understanding, and humour
- PJ McDonald and his outstanding faculty and staff at Eagle Hill, who not only prepared Andrew and Ainsley for the future but gave David and me four years of respite
- Kiaras Gharabaghi at Toronto Metropolitan University, who believed in Ainsley and turned potential failure into memorable success

To the Toronto Blue Jays, who played an instrumental role not only in getting Andrew through his darkest days but in giving him such joy (except when Carlos Delgado left!)

To the Rogers Communications' team, who embrace inclusion and diversity and role-model what it means to understand, accommodate, and value developmentally disabled and autistic employees. As part of this thanks, the guidance of Ready, Willing and Able has been invaluable.

And to our personal angels:

- David's and my families, as well as to those friends who have stood by us and supported us. They have seen us when we could barely function and when we despaired of ever having a happy life. They have stuck by us, and I love them for it.
- Daniel Glazerman, as well as Don Fraser, who have willingly

taken on their future guardianship and/or executor roles without reservation; we know this is no small task!

- Zakir Jaffer, who has been a remarkable mentor to Andrew, both professionally and personally, and who has agreed to be a key advisor in the future
- Sue Rosborough, who taught Andrew the benefits of supported independent living, and Dennis O'Keeffe, who provided much-needed male levity and play punching
- Mentors Stephen Bloom, Cam Dunbar, and Russell Spencer, who have given Andrew and Ainsley valued guidance and life lessons and kicked them both in the teeth from time to time
- Stu Eley, Rick Arsenault, and Rob Johnson, who have shown great friendship and kindness to Andrew; they are models of law enforcement

To Dr. Peter Szatmari of SickKids and CAMH, who wrote such a thoughtful and compelling Foreword and positioned *Hold on Tight* in such a skillful manner.

To Sarah Scott at Barlow Books as well as Tracy Bordian, Christina Palassio, Wendy Thomas, and Lena Yang. As a first-time author, I would not have been able to complete this book without their guidance.

To Heidi Sander at DigiWriting, who expertly coached me on digital promotion and brought me into the 21st century.

To authors Georgie Binks, Ian Brown, and Katherine Govier, who gave me valued advice that started me on my publishing journey.

To my husband, David, who has been my rock and partner throughout this roller-coaster journey. We are a great team. He picks me up, provides me with needed balance, and reminds me to laugh. My gratitude and love are endless.

And to my incredible children, Andrew and Ainsley. They inspire me every day. This book is a love song to them.

INDEX

ABOUT THE AUTHOR

Jan Stewart is a highly regarded mental health governance expert and advocate. Her brutally honest memoir, *Hold on Tight: A Parent's Journey Raising Children with Mental Illness*, describes her emotional roller coaster story parenting two children with multiple, complex mental health disorders. Her mission is to empower and inspire parents to persevere, as well as to better educate their families, friends, health care professionals, educators, and employers on the parental perspective. Jan chairs the Board of Directors at Kerry's Place Autism Services, Canada's largest autism services provider, and was previously vice chair at the Centre for Addiction and Mental Health. She spent most of her career as a senior partner with the global executive search firm Egon Zehnder. Jan is a Diamond Life Master in bridge and enjoys fitness, genealogy, and dance.